Tales of Old Wallingford

1670–1970

CLARENCE E. HALE

Globe
Pequot

Guilford, Connecticut

Published by Globe Pequot
An imprint of The Rowman & Littlefield Publishing Group, Inc.
4501 Forbes Boulevard, Suite 200, Lanham, Maryland 20706
www.rowman.com

Unit A, Whitacre Mews, 26-34 Stannary Street, London SE11 4AB

Distributed by NATIONAL BOOK NETWORK

British Library Cataloguing in Publication Information Available

LCCCN 70-175812
ISBN 978-1-4930-3315-7 (paper : alk. paper)
ISBN 978-1-4930-3316-4 (electronic)

♾️™ The paper used in this publication meets the minimum requirements of
American National Standard for Information Sciences—Permanence of Paper
for Printed Library Materials, ANSI/NISO Z39.48-1992.

Printed in the United States of America

To   Ruth
for her sufferance
that this book might be born

Foreword

In presenting these "Tales of Old Wallingford" I have endeavored to recount briefly in the historical articles the events of importance to the people of the town in the sequence of events from the founding in 1670 to the celebration of the tercentenary in 1970.

It is my hope that the sketches which interlard the historical accounts will serve to give a New England flavor to the book, as well as an occasional relieving touch of humor. The stories, by the way, all have an actual historical basis of character or situation, though the names may have been altered.

In the preparation of the material, I wish to acknowledge my debt to the late Mrs. Clara Booth Newell for the voluminous historical data laboriously gathered together over many years. In the chapter on "The Wallingford Disaster" I have used general information from the book of that title by John B. Kendrick. The standard history of Wallingford and Meriden of Dr. Charles H. S. Davis, published just one hundred years ago, has also proved a valuable source.

I am particularly indebted to the *Wallingford Post*, where most of this material has appeared over the last several years, for assistance in the preparation of the typography.

If the work serves to acquaint the thousands of our citizens who have become residents in the last quarter century with Wallingford's past, I shall be especially pleased.

CLARENCE E. HALE

Contents

CHAPTER 1

The Quinnipiacs

The Quinnipiac tribe of Indians, living in the environs of New Haven harbor and the mouth of the Quinnipiac River was a relatively small group, affiliated with the larger tribe of Mattabesetts of Middletown. The Quinnipiacs had lived for a long time in constant fear of raids from their powerful neighbors, the Pequots on the East around New London and the Mohawks who made occasional forays from the Hudson Valley. Actually there were only forty-seven able bodied warriors in the Quinnipiac tribe at that time.

Learning of the English settlements at Hartford and Windsor, the Quinnipiacs sent word that they would welcome English settlers at New Haven to serve as protectors against their warlike neighbors. So when Davenport, Eaton and their associates arrived, they were warmly greeted and the purchase in 1638 from Momauguin of the New Haven harbor area and territory extending several miles North was quickly and amicably arranged. The tribe withdrew to a reservation in the present East Haven section and continued as before their life of hunting, fishing and raising corn and beans.

Only a few months after their purchase from Momauguin, Davenport and Eaton purchased from Montowese a block of land extending ten miles North of the New Haven lands and thirteen miles in breadth — eight miles East from the Quinnipiac River and five miles West. During the next 30 years, as the New Haven

Colony gained in members and strength, similar purchases were made along the shore and settlements were established at Branford, Guilford, Milford, Fairfield and Stamford. It was only natural, then, that the next thrust of settlement should be into the wilderness to the North along the crude path to Hartford.

Accordingly in 1669 a committee of interested persons was appointed to look into the feasibility of establishing a settlement up the Quinnipiac and a site of high land — the present Main Street — was selected. It is certain that a few adventurous men were already living in the boundaries of present Wallingford including Abraham Doolittle, John Peck, John Moss and John Brockett and these men composed the vanguard of the group who made the permanent settlement in 1670, as a "plantation" of the New Haven Colony.

It was against this background of history and environment that probably in the spring of 1670, the 38 founders of Wallingford and their families moved from New Haven up the Old Colony Rd. to where Cedar St. meets Colony at the Iron Bridge and then up the present Parsons St. to the section between present Parsons St. and Ward St. Wallingford was now born, but still an infant as the New Haven Committee continued to exercise overall authority for some years.

In that same year, the Court of Election in Hartford confirmed the action of New Haven in setting the following boundaries for Wallingford:

From the point where Wharton's Brook empties into the Quinnipiac East to a point South of Pistapaug Reservoir where it meets the Branford line, then ten miles North along the Middletown line to the present area of Mt. Higby, then West to approximately present Milldale, and South including present Cheshire to the Sleeping Giant, thence East to the Quinnipiac and point of departure.

CHAPTER 2

The Founding

In April 1670, the original 38 settlers of
Wallingford with their families moved from New
Haven, and in a few instances from other towns, to
Wallingford. Their coming had been preceded in
1668 by Abraham Doolittle and John Peck and in
1669 by John Moss and John Brockett, and these
men acted as a committee for the settlement.
Probably in that period, John Brockett, who as a
surveyor had laid out the famous nine squares in
New Haven comprising the green and surrounding
streets, had made a rough survey of the projected
village, and perhaps gone so far as to indicate the
division into house lots and streets. There seems to
have been no hesitancy on agreement about the
general layout of the "Long Highway," now Main
Street, and the cross streets.

These men found this region a wilderness.
Present Main Street was heavily forested with oak,
chestnut, hickory, elm, pine, hemlock and the
various trees native to New England. Wolves by the
thousand roamed the woods along with numerous
deer, bear, smaller animals, and, of course, wild
turkey, quail and partridge. The Wharton Brook area
was an almost impassable swamp. To the west, it
seems probable that the "Great Plain" presented
much the same appearance as it does today in those
places not taken over by the bull-dozer, factories,

roads, shopping centers and parking lots. Thus, these first settlers faced physical dangers from wild beasts, possible Indian incursions, and the lesser but ever present evils of cold, disease, accident, and, of course, unremitting toil.

The first house lots were laid out on the east side of the "Long Highway" from about Parsons Street to present Ward Street, and consisted of six acres each extending back to Wharton Brook. The present Ward Street was laid out from Main Street east to the brook and west to the river.

The next house lots, also of six acres, were laid out on both sides of the highway from Ward Street to present Center Street. Here again the cross street extended from brook to river, and provision was made for the "training ground" or green and for a "Ministry Site" on the corner, now as for nearly three hundred years the location of the First Congregational Church.

Similar house lots were laid out and assigned extending up the highway to another cross street called Mix Lane, now Christian Street, and finally to the top of the "Long Highway" and the cross street, now North Street. In succeeding years allotments of acreage were made along the Quinnipiac for pasturage and other uses.

It is an interesting fact that for nearly 200 years Wallingford, as such, existed simply as Main Street and Elm Streets. My mother told me that when she was a little girl around 1860 there was not a single building on Center Street between Main Street and the railroad station, and a print I have showing a view of the town from the railroad station confirms her statement. There were, of course, occasional houses scattered about in the plains area.

Building homes for shelter, clearing the land, raising what crops were possible and just getting organized as a community provided the necessity for Herculean labors in the years from 1670 to 1675.

when King Philip's War brought about a brief but dramatic interruption of progress. Such an event was a fearful situation because these people were isolated to a degree which it is impossible for us to realize. Now a man can be on the moon or in the depths of the seas, but he can communicate with the world at large. While Wallingford was only 12 miles from New Haven, it would take hours to get there and back, assuming conditions permitted anyone to escape from the settlement, and Hartford was a day's journey away. In accident or sickness no skilled medical help was available. Wolves, wild cats and other animals skulked about seeking out unprotected sheep and other domestic animals, so much so that a town meeting set a bounty on all that could be killed. For this action perhaps the unearthly howling at night was more responsible than the loss of the animals.

There was so much that had to be done all at once. It was necessary to have a grist mill to grind the corn, and after great effort a man from Stratford was persuaded to come and set up one at "Quinnie." Religion was a highly important factor in the life of the people, and from the first services were held in the homes of Ensign Munson and Lieutenant Merriman. In 1673, the Rev. Samuel Street became the first minister. His household goods were brought up by boat to a dock near North Haven and then carried by ox-cart to the house provided for him at 238 So. Main St., now the residence of Robert Thompson.

Because of interruptions and changes in plans, it was not until five years later that a small church or more properly descriptive "meeting house" since it was used not only for religious services but for other public assemblies was built. Accordingly, a log structure, temporary in nature until a more suitable and permanent church could be provided for the "Ministry Site," was erected on the common directly opposite Stimpson's drug store. During my boyhood,

this exact spot was the site of the bandstand, where
for more than a quarter of a century such worthies
as Burr Hall and "Rod" Austin delighted the
populace on Saturday evenings with classical and
popular airs.

CHAPTER 3

The Founders

The original group of Wallingford settlers consisted of 36 men, 34 women and 56 children. The oldest member of this company was Mrs. Katherine Miles, who was 82. One can imagine her leaving her old home in New Haven, being driven to a dock on the Quinnipiac estuary, and then brought by boat up to the dock in North Haven. The name given to that place, "Bogmire Dock," indicates these people were not lacking in grim humor. From North Haven she and her household effects were brought probably by ox-cart over the plains to Wallingford. She was the mother-in-law of Reverend Samuel Street. That she lived to be 95 indicates she was a tough old lady.

Prominent in the affairs of the town both before and after settlement in 1670 was John Moss. Indeed it was he who was probably responsible for the naming, as his home in England was near Wallingford on the Thames. He was the oldest man in the group at 66 years of age, and had been a signer of the original New Haven Covenant in 1638. As first magistrate of the town he performed the first wedding. All these facts tell the kind of man he was, but perhaps the best proof is that he waited until he was 100 years old before making his will and finally died at 103.

John Brockett, to whom reference has already been made, was in a sense the first city planner in the country, and his fame still lives. He had established himself prior to 1670 on land at the South boundary near Wharton's brook. It is a very happy fact that the family name appears today frequently in the press in announcing marriages and new generations.

Abraham Doolittle, the founder of the very large and active Doolittle family in the United States, was 49 years old in 1670. He, too, had explored the territory prior to 1670 and was a prime mover in urging and bringing about the settlement. He held many town offices and with Moss, Brockett and Merriman held the leadership in all civic affairs.

Although John Beach never resided here, he left a square mile of land on the west side, some of which remained in the same family until recent years. It is still known as the Beach farm, and Zera Beach was a well known local farmer in my boyhood.

Joseph Benham is remembered because his wife and 13-year-old daughter were accused of witchcraft right here in Wallingford. They were adjudged innocent by the court in Hartford in the last trial for witchcraft in New England.

Samuel Cook was the first tanner and shoemaker. The name has been prominent in the affairs of the town for three hundred years and is carried on such landmarks as Cook Hill, and the Cook farm on the Northford Road, kept in the same family with its beautiful ancestral home for many generations.

Ensign Thomas Curtis, distinguished for bravery in King Philip's War, Captain Samuel Hall, grandfather of Lyman Hall, Daniel Hooper who didn't disdain a grant of 12 acres at "Dog's Misery" a swampy area in the northeastern section, now part of Meriden, and many others did their part in the early life of the settlement.

Such were some of the men who founded the town and were the ancestors of many living here today. Perhaps the prevalence of Halls is due to the good start furnished by the three Hall brothers, sons of Captain Samuel, who accounted for a total of 26 children! But what of the 34 women, brave and strong, too, but unsung and rarely mentioned? If this settlement in the wilderness was tough for the men, it was tougher for the women, who had to face the same hardships, certainly equal toil, and in addition the worries, dangers and suffering of childbirth with no help beyond a kindly neighbor to act as midwife.

Who can picture the agonized mind of Mrs. Samuel Potter as she faced the birth of her baby, the first in Wallingford in 1671? Who can imagine the tortured soul of Mrs. Eleazur Peck whose little boy was the first to die in Wallingford in 1673? During the few years following 1670 72 babies were born in Wallingford. Were the men brave, then can less by said of the women?

Our history shows that women succumbed much sooner to these conditions than men, and there are records of many second and even third marriages with each wife leaving a complement of children to the next. And what sadder fate does a woman face than to leave her children to be brought up by another? By all means sing the prowess of the men, but to overlook the women's part is to fail utterly to appreciate the hardships of our forbears in their most heartrending manifestations.

CHAPTER 4

The Leaders

What manner of men were these who braved the terrors and loneliness of the wilderness to found our town? That they were brave goes without saying. They were also hardy, industrious, intelligent, well versed in all kinds of handicrafts and trades, and deeply religious to the point of fanaticism. It must be constantly kept in mind in evaluating the events of the period and the men and women that the Puritans, some 20,000 in number, left for the most part comfortable homes in England to face a dangerous voyage of weeks and sometimes months with every possible discomfort and risk of disease and accident and then in addition all the uncertainties and hardships of the wilderness, because they rebelled against and refused to accept the innovations, the corruption, and the rituals of the established Church of England.

Because they were leaders in the community and because many of the old families in town are direct descendants, Lieutenant Nathaniel Merriman and the Rev. Samuel Street are of special interest. The former, then 57 years old, had left London as a young man of perhaps 19, and made his way to New Haven where the records show him active in military and civic affairs. Prior to this he had fought in the Pequot War from Hartford. So it was natural that from the first settlers of Wallingford he was chosen as commander of the "Train

Band" for protection against the Indians, and he was officially confirmed in 1672 by the General Court. Although a constant guard was maintained and two houses were fully fortified, his own at the northwest corner of Main and Ward Streets and Rev. Mr. Street's, no actual struggle with the Indians ever took place in Wallingford. He remained as commander until 1692 when he ceased his military career at the age of 78.

During those years he was representative from Wallingford at the General Court in Hartford for nine sessions; served as juror and commissioner on boundaries and bridges; for nine years he was town clerk; altogether an influential leader. When in 1675 King Philip's War broke out, all New England was panic stricken for it was obvious the Indians were determined to exterminate the white settlers. Although 62 years old, he was appointed Captain of Dragoons for New Haven County. As such he seems to have participated in the Great Swamp fight at South Kingston, R.I., where some 300 Connecticut troops were engaged, and where his son, Nathaniel Jr., was killed. In recognition of these services the town voted him 10 acres of land and to Nathaniel's brothers five acres each.

The evidence is clear that he was brave and efficient and faithful in the many tasks entrusted to him. His records as town clerk still attest his neatness and accuracy. His will devising property of a value of 557 British pounds, a very respectable estate, is a model of careful thought and fairness of judgment, making sure that his "beloved wife (receive) the bed, bolster and pillows with a pair of the best sheets, the best rug and blanket, the curtains and vallanse, together with the bedstead, all which we have usually reposed in during the time of our living together." It is obvious he wished to make certain she would not have to sleep on the floor, cold and unprotected! His descendants can take pride in this record of a strong man, meeting all the vicissitudes of a long life of almost constant activity from the streets of London to the wilderness of the New World with fortitude and complete fidelity to the trust placed in him.

For 45 years the Rev. Samuel Street was the spiritual leader of the community. In 1673 the settlers at great sacrifice built the house at 238 So. Main St. Mr. Street was a graduate of Harvard in the class of 1664, a period when the entire college enrollment numbered 23 young men, an excellent example of the primary purpose of the establishment of the college "for the education of young men for the ministry" with the motto "Christo et Ecclesiae" (for Christ and the Church). His influence among the first settlers was very great both in spiritual and civic affairs, and he set an example of long and devoted service to our Congregational Church which has served as a beacon light for those succeeding him.

CHAPTER 5

Seventeenth Century Houses

The only houses constructed in the 17th century and still standing on Main St. are the Samuel Street house at 238 So. Main St., the Jeremiah How house on the corner of Main and Christian St., and the Nehemiah Royce house, originally on the northeast corner of North St. and Main, but moved over 30 years ago to the west side of Main St. opposite Dutton Park. Other 17th century houses are the Dr. John Hull house at the head of Main St. extension at Barnes Rd. and the house in Pond Hill brought in knocked down by the late Elmer Keith and re-erected opposite the old brick house

During the first two years after settlement, Mr. John Harriman, though not an ordained minister, preached on the Sabbath to the people. In 1672, the Rev. Samuel Street, son of the New Haven pastor, was invited to settle in Wallingford as the permanent pastor and on Feb. 24, 1673 "it was ordered that Mr. Street's house be raised at the Townes charge." In April 1673 a town meeting appointed a committee to "fetch Mr. Street's goods from New Haven and land them where they may be carted to Wallingford." The spot probably was "Bogmire Dock" in North Haven to which point they were brought by barge from New Haven up the Quinnipiac and thence by ox-cart.

Apparently the work of building the house lagged for the very good reason that each man of the few available was intensively engaged by his own problems.

It was voted to let out the timber and stone work "to such as will take it." Apparently none would, so orders went out "if none take it, then the work be committed to four overseers." These overseers were empowered "to call forth suitable men to work. Every man according to his proportion until it be finished according to the town's engagement to Mr. Street."

Whatever the difficulties encountered, however loath the harried men were to sacrifice their own necessities to erect the parsonage, the fact remains that the structure built was so sturdy that today it stands as sound and strong as the day it was finished nearly 300 years ago.

As Davis writes in his history of Wallingford: "It may serve to convey some idea of the character of the people that when their own poor dwellings were hardly erected and they were struggling with the untold difficulties of a wilderness, and when their whole number, men, women and children, hardly exceeded one hundred," they accomplished such a feat. Lacking money, having no excess of crops to sell, the town voted that its people take to the swamps and cut 1500 pipestaves, which had a ready trade value in New Haven for shipment to the West Indies for rum barrels, to provide funds for materials for the house not available from forest and quarry. In this house Mr. Street and his family lived for the entire 42 years of his pastorate. What men and women these were!

Jeremiah How was one of the 38 men who signed the original Wallingford covenant and was allotted lot No. 11 of six acres on the southeast corner of Main and Christian Sts. There he built the house which serves as usefully today as a home, as it has for close to 300 years.

Nehemiah Royce, or as the name was frequently spelled Rise or Rice, was admitted to reside in the community by vote of the committee empowered to pass on all newcomers on Feb. 12, 1671. No one was allowed to take up residence in Wallingford by purchase or otherwise except with the consent of this committee after it had secured "sufficient testimony of their good conversation in the place where they formerly lived." (Conversation in its archaic meaning of behavior or manner of living.)

Having passed the test for admission, Royce was allotted plot No. 17 on the northeast corner of Main and North Sts. The house was occupied by many generations of the Royce family and Mrs. Hale's great-great-grandmother, Rachel Royce, was married from there. It was indeed most fitting that the last private occupant was Miss Helen Royce. Several years ago the Choate School, at great expense, had the house completely renovated for use as a guest house so it may now be expected to last another three centuries.

As Davis states in his history of Wallingford, "Their poverty in this world rendered them unable for many years to do much more than provide mean shelters for their families" so it is quite possible that when Nehemiah Royce came to Wallingford in 1671, he built on his lot a small dwelling. At a later date when labor and materials were in larger supply he would have built the large salt box type house and added his original small house to it as a kitchen ell. When I sold the salt box to Miss Royce in 1927 my father-in-law purloined the ell for his workshop and it is still at the rear of the Rogers residence next to the Cleborne house which stands on the original site of the Royce house.

If this theory be historically accurate — and certainly the customary salt box house does not have an ell — then the Royce house by consanguinity and long association with the ell may be characterized as the oldest house in town. Otherwise, the thoroughly documented records would seem to bestow that distinction on the Street house.

CHAPTER 6

King Philip's War

Hardly had the Wallingford settlers established their rude homes, cleared some fields for crops, and set up an ecclesiastical and civil government than they were faced with a crisis which threatened to wipe out all they had accomplished and possibly their lives as well.

Relations between the Indians of Rhode Island and the English had been deteriorating for years. The English constantly pressed in on the hunting and fishing grounds, and sought to subject the Indians in their activities to English law and customs. Finally, driven by desperation, Nanuntenoo, chief of the Wampanoag tribe, called King Philip by the English, in the belief that the only recourse left was to exterminate the English, attacked the town of Swansey and in quick succession Taunton, Middleboro and Dartmouth.

Instantly, all New England was on the alert for possible Indian raids. Wallingford was in an isolated and exposed position with only a rough path or trail to New Haven and Hartford and open to the East by trails to the Connecticut River Valley. Accordingly, on Aug. 27, 1675, the town voted:

"In respect to the present danger of the Indians it was ordered that the inhabitants secure themselves and the principall of theyre goods by fortifying about two houses which houses are to be Mr. Samuel Street's and Lieutenant Merriman's and that this work of fortifying be set upon the 28th of August by the whole town and followed until it be effected and whosever fails to pay a fine of five shillings."

Further resolutions followed ordering every man to bring arms and ammunition to Sunday meeting, setting up a four man guard on Sunday, and two men to watch all day and two men all night. In September after the first panic had subsided the watch was reduced, but at the same period provision was made to fortify out of the town treasury the exposed Southern end of town and as late as March 1676 the town was still appointing a committee to review the fortifications.

These fortifications consisted of palisades of heavy timbers placed in deep trenches. The firearms were of two kinds, the matchlock and fire lock. The former was fired by a wick of twisted cotton or thread soaked in rum and filled with fine powder wound on a reel attached to the gun The gun itself had a very long barrel with a wide mouth, so long and heavy, a "rest" was required, consisting of a rod pointed on one end to thrust in the ground and with a crotch in the other in which the gun rested so it could be aimed accurately. The firelocks used flints, shot and powder, but were less accurate. The colonists also used swords and long steel pointed wooden pikes.

In November 1675, Nathaniel Merriman was appointed Captain of Dragoons for the New Haven area which was to furnish sixty men for the campaign against the Narragansetts which culminated in the Great Swamp Fight on the 19th of December 1675, as ferocious and cruel a battle as has ever been fought on American soil. The colonists suffered heavy losses including Nathaniel Merriman's son. Some three hundred Indians were slain and an equal number taken prisoner, the Indian fort was burned to ashes and hundreds of Indian women and children turned out to shift for themselves in the middle of winter.

While this battle broke the back of the Indian uprising, Philip refused to make peace, and stray bands of Indians continued to wreck havoc on the countryside. There were attacks on Deerfield, Hadley and Springfield, whereupon the colonists organized a large force, and succeeded in rooting out the last of the Indian resistance. In these operations, Merriman and his men seem to have taken active part.

Although Wallingford was not directly attacked, the Cole house in present Meriden was burned, a Mr. Kirby of Middletown was murdered, and as Merriman wrote on March 30, 1676, concerning roving Indians: "These things being considered we do judge the enemie is near us and desire you speedily send us some help." By the middle of 1676, the danger was over, and henceforth Wallingford remained free of any anxiety at the hands of its original inhabitants so it could devote all its energies to building for the future.

Of Wallingford's 40 men, many old, Merriman in his 60's, eight served in King Philip's War and this established the tradition of patriotism which has been evident in every such call to arms in the past three hundred years. The Indian Nanuntenoo, or King Philip, was the prototype of the noble red man. Within the scope of his birth and traditions he was a brave and skillful leader who foresaw that the Indian race was doomed unless it could once and for all stop the encroachment of the Colonists and drive them from the shores of New England. When tracked down and captured by men of his own race and dragged before his white enemies he refused all overtures to save his life by making peace, and in words equal in nobility of sentiment to those of Socrates before he took the hemlock or Nathan Hale at the foot of the gibbet, he said:

"I like it well. I shall die before my heart is soft or I have said anything unworthy of myself."

So he died at the hands of Uncas, whose father had killed Massasoit, Philip's father. Such was the savagery of the times in which Wallingford was born.

CHAPTER 7

The Yankee

Recently while reading a rather ancient book on the travels in the United States of an English lady, Mrs. Frances Trollope, I came across the following passage: "Though not in Yankee or New England territory we were near enough to meet many delightful specimens of this most peculiar race. It is by no means rare to meet people who push acuteness to the verge of honesty, but the Yankee is the only one to boast of it. In shrewdness, cautiousness, industry and perseverance he resembles the Scotch; in habits of frugal neatness, the Dutch; in love of lucre, the sons of Abraham, but in frank admission and superlative admiration of his own peculiarities, he stands supreme."

Of the above passage it may be said, as Mark Twain wrote, "Of all foreign commentators on American manners, Mrs. Trollope alone dealt what the gamblers call a strictly 'square game.' She did not gild us, neither did she whitewash us."

Like the whooping crane, the simon-pure New England Yankee as a distinctive breed is fast disappearing. One is more apt to find a purer strain in the Middle West, though small pockets still exist in the remote sections of Maine, New Hampshire and Vermont. As I-91 and other parkways bore North these last bastions are doomed to fall to the mixed lineage of the cities.

Just what is a Yankee? The derivation of the word

is unknown, but it was coined by the British soldiers —
perhaps the Hessians from the Dutch "Janke" meaning
Little John — as a term of derision for the ragged and
unkempt rabble that fought them at Bennington and
Saratoga. The word has been used to cover all
Americans by the British, and all Northerners by the
Confederates in the Civil War, though in the latter case
the word was always hyphenated into damn-Yankee.

If I may be permitted to define the name, I would
say a pure bred Yankee is one whose ancestry on both
sides is of English stock and prior to 1700. Essentially,
this reduces the original group to the Puritan movement
from England to America in the period following 1620.
The characteristics of those relatively few thousands of
people provide the natural clues to the qualities faults,
and especially the peculiarities as set forth by Mrs.
Trollope.

In the 16th century there was an awakening of
spiritual life in England based on Wycliff's Bible as
preached by the Lollards, the influence of John Calvin,
and the growth of the Puritan movement. Persecuted by
Crown and Church, many Puritans fled to Holland,
while the movement persisted and grew in England.
When finally the way was cleared for these troublesome
Puritans to be permanently removed from infecting
more Englishment, the emigration from the Low
Countries and England began and continued for the
next 50 to 75 years.

These were people of deep religious convictions
who had suffered greatly because of them and were
prepared to undergo far worse. They did not cross the
Atlantic to improve their worldly condition which had
been perfectly comfortable. "All, perhaps without a
single exception," says de Tocqueville, "had received a
good education, and as a group possessed in proportion
to their number a greater mass of intelligence than is to
be found in any European nation in our own time
(1835). They were driven by a purely intellectual
craving, and their object was the triumph of an idea."

This idea was the construction of a theocratic state which should be for Christians all that the theocracy of Moses had been for the Jews in Old Testament history. Sin was to be abolished by law. An outrage offered by son to parents was punishable by death, not to say such peccadilloes as blasphemy, sorcery, adultery and rape. The Connecticut "Blue Laws" formulated by my early grandfather penalized the man who kissed his wife on Sunday, and another forbear signed in Hartford in 1638 an "information" accusing a woman of witchcraft.

The Yankee has such non-sense for his background, but the next century set the seal on his character. In brief, this consisted of enduring the hardships encountered in merely staying alive, in gradually pushing his way inland from the Coast through the wilderness, of savage wars with the Indians and the fear of raids, of religious and political controversies, and threats from the Dutch in the West and the French on the North.

Is it to be wondered that the Yankee emerged as a "peculiar race." He had to be acute and cautious to survive. The old stone walls still to be found winding through deep forests over mountain and swamp are proof of his industry and perseverance. His dire poverty ingrained in bone, sinew and consciousness that frugality that becomes penuriousness in more affluent times. Any humor that could be extracted from a life of constant toil and hardships was bound to be wry and dry.

But here also were sown the seeds of inventive genius. The Yankee, isolated on his farm, had to devise ways and means, tools and contraptions to meet his needs. One has only to look at Eric Sloane's books to marvel at his ingenuity. On this foundation rests the industrial history of New England.

The Yankee is not a dreamer. He takes things as he finds them and makes the best of them that he can. This makes him less temperamental, more even tempered, less ebullient when things go well, less downcast when everything goes wrong. He is a middle of the roader, finding there the smoothest path and the least possibility of attack by man or beast. There, too, it is easier to move to right or left as circumstances warrant.

Psychologically, he is most at ease when he rests firmly on the past, and prods cautiously into the future. As a speculator he is a flat failure, and as a leader of causes, since Abolitionist days, he has found nothing to get excited about. He would rather miss winning the prize than risk falling on his face. He is firm on his feet, steadfast in his opinions, and because he has a feeling for the past, sure he is right. All this is very trying for others of more mercurial temperament, momentary enthusiasms, and reckless action. He is as hard to move as a boulder in his pasture without the fulcrum of logic and the oxteam and sled of history.

A Yankee not only keeps his feelings to himself — he buries them. My own grandfather, then 75 years old and childless, wrote in his diary on Sept. 30, 1857: "My first child was born today about 3 o'clock in the afternoon." Where the joy, the rapture, the hallelujahs? And where any mention of the comely widow whom he had married in his old age? As a Yankee he duly set down the fact and the time. The "my" may have reflected the proclivity to boast as reported by Mrs. Trollope, and it was a rather remarkable performance.

Without his sense of humor, the Yankee would be a rather dull fellow. It is a dry wit, rarely mordant or caustic, and draws its point from situations rather than personalities. Illustrative stories are numberless. While visiting my Uncle Delano one day on his farm I was watching him at work in his barn when I noticed several large holes in the roof through which a brilliant sun was shining. When I called his attention to them, he asked, "Ain't getting wet, are you, Clarence? If you are, step over this way." I assured him I was not, but wondered why he didn't repair them. Looking up in a contemplative manner, he said, "I mean to, but there's no harm leaving them today, and when it rains I can't work on the roof."

A similar philosophical attitude toward life was inherited by his son, my cousin Walter. Some years before an apple tree in his yard had been blown down and rested on its side. I asked why he didn't cut it up for fire wood. Looking at me in a quizzical way, he drawled, "There's so many things on a farm that have to be done like milking that it's kind of relaxing to have something to look at that don't."

However, my favorite is about the small boy who was asked by a passing motorist if he knew the way to Boston.

"Nope," said the boy.

"Well, can you direct me to Nashua."

"Nope," said the boy.

Exasperated, the motorist asked, "Don't you know anything?"

"Nope," said the boy. "But I ain't lost."

As I look over the list of high school graduates, the obvious Yankee names are buried among their Italian, Polish, Hungarian, Jewish and various national counterparts with a recent infusion of Spanish. Occasionally, I see a Yankee name, but the girl named Brockett may have lustrous dark eyes and a cream and roses cheek from generations under the Italian sun, and the boy may have a brachycephalic skull. My own grandchildren have French, Jewish and perhaps other strains I know not what. I have a hunch a Scandinavian is coming up.

But whether the names of future generations be Orzechowski, Jorgensen, Lanouette, Feinblum, or Biancioni, among those qualities of Italian love of life and beauty, French vivacity and pure reason, Jewish tenacity, resiliency and ethical culture, and the ardor for freedom of the Pole or Hungarian, I believe there will be an occasional throwback to the Yankee, including, I hope, some of his virtues.

CHAPTER 8

Wallingford Divided

The century between King Philips War and the Revolution was, as might be expected, one of quiet growth and development of agricultural resources on the one hand and a tumultuous civil and political life on the other. It was a period of road and bridge building as incoming settlers extended their farms and habitations around the countryside. In professional circles appeared physicians and lawyers. Workers in metals, blacksmiths and tinsmiths, harness and bootmakers set up shop, all necessary to the burgeoning growth of the community.

Almost from the first, Cheshire struggled to become a separate town because its people found the distance to church and school almost prohibitive. As early as 1711, a composition was effected as to the school problem, and in 1724 it was set off as a separate parish with its own minister. It was not, however, until 1780 that Cheshire was formally divorced from Wallingford and was incorporated as a separate township.

With the 40 families in Meriden in 1725, Wallingford was even more grudging, and having lost Cheshire in 1780, it clung to Meriden until 1806. To this recalcitrance on the part of Wallingford the lack of empathy that the succeeding centuries have glossed over but never eradicated may be due.

The first settlers undeniably had their virtues but they were a contentious lot, constantly quarreling and bickering and "going to law" among themselves. The immediate cause was land Having set up their homes on the original six acres, they began to reach out for the best land in the outskirts, and naturally that most eagerly sought was that capable of returning an immediate income. One product in great and constant demand was pipe-staves and hoops. These were taken to New Haven whence sloops took them to the West Indies. There they were formed into barrels for rum and molasses exchanged by the Yankee traders for salt codfish and other "civilized" goods.

Accordingly the land which. bordered on and included the swamps around Wallingford where this raw material grew was first seized upon in grants from the town, and this is probably the first instance in its history of the workings of political pull. It is recorded that even the ministers – who were also, of course, farmers on the side – got into the act and the Rev. Samuel Street seems to have received his share at least.

It would appear that the swamp which had the most and perhaps the best material for pipe staves and hoops was that known as "Dogs Misery" so named because dogs pursuing animals amid its briars and muck came out very much the worse for wear. This swamp lay in the area south of the road from Meriden to Middletown around Black Pond and extending about a mile south, land now constituting the Industrial Park and site of the International Silver Co.'s new plant. Disputes among grantees of land in this area waxed furious, including a famous law suit between Dr. John Hull, Wallingford's first physician, and Isaac Curtis. The high value attached to this land is also indicated by the fact that Nathaniel Royce left his daughter as her portion "three and one half acres at Dogs Misery."

For 70 years there were no wars that affected Wallingford, but ten men died in the siege of Louisbourg and dozens fought in the French and Indian War of 1755-62 at Ticonderoga and Quebec.

In civic affairs, the grasp of the Congregational

Church on the life of the town both ecclesiastical and civil, stemming from the Fundamental Orders of 1638, was gradually loosened. In 1735, some ten families organized a Baptist church society. This gave rise to much argument and many ecclesiastical squabbles, and in Saybrook some Baptists were arrested, fined and thrown into jail. By the year 1750, the congregation had dissolved, not to be reestablished for 50 years.

Similarly in 1745, several families joined to form a parish of the Church of England. This religious sect was seemingly more acceptable to the Congregationalists, probably from the historic connection, and in 1752 Reverend Ichabod Camp became rector and a church was erected in 1758.

The loosening of old restraints and of the autocratic rule of the Congregational Church was apparent in the Act of Toleration of 1708 by which Episcopal form of worship was allowed. The famous "Dana Controversy" not only shook Wallingford to the very foundations of its civil and religious life, but all New England. It resulted in a split in the Congregational Church and formation of the Wells Society. It took 30 years and a new pastor for this to heal.

It was not until almost 100 years later that the immigration from Ireland brought members of the Catholic faith to Wallingford. Walking to New Haven and back to Mass was too great a hardship, and in 1847 the first Mass was celebrated at the home of James Hanlon on the corner of Main and High streets. The first Catholic school was established in the home of Martin Owens on Elm St. in 1851.

CHAPTER 9

The Dana Controversy

In order to understand the tremendous impact of the Dana Controversy on ecclesiastical and civil life in Wallingford and throughout New England, it is necessary to have a preliminary briefing on the Fundamental Orders of 1638, and the Roger Ludlow Code of 1650. The former provided the fundamental laws of Connecticut for about one hundred years, and a substantial portion of the latter was in effect until 1900.

Following the settlement of Windsor, Hartford, and Wethersfield, the leaders of these communities soon realized that isolated as they were it was necessary to have a general agreement or covenant outlining the regulations by which they could live under law. The express purpose of this covenant, however, was to provide a civil government to cooperate with the ecclesiastical authorities in the preservation of the rule of the Congregational Church. In fact the civil government was set up to serve the role of law enforcement for the church.

Because servants, apprentices, women and many newcomers were not church members and therefore ineligible to vote, only approximately one-third of the people had a voice in the civil government, and in general the leaders and officers of the churches were the same men who constituted the civil authority. In short, the Congregational Church had things buttoned up tight for nearly one hundred years.

However, as the population increased and new generations matured, the church was gradually forced to relinquish its arbitrarv. autocratic and theocratic rule. This is hardly to be wondered at when it is considered that the code catalogued 23 offenses punishable by death including witchcraft, blasphemy, idolatry, and more usual crimes including the refusal of any youth over, not under, 16 who refused to obey his parents. The idea that any child under 16 would disobey was incomprehensible, or at least could be dealt with in summary fashion. It is fair to add that there is no record of any execution for such insubordination so probably the threat had the effect intended. Perhaps parents today in some instances would like to have the old law reconstituted with the hope of similar results!

It is a fact that ordinary crimes and many irksome church dictated regulations were harshly administered with repeated whippings, confinement in the stocks and fines. However, the incursion of settlers from England, members of the Church of England, resulted in the Act of Toleration of 1708, which permitted organization and worship under that sect, and other sects like the Baptists began battling for similar recognition.

Accordingly, by the middle of the 18th century the grip of the Congregational Church on the lives of the people had been loosened, and in fact, it had to turn to contend with new and seemingly heretical divisions in its own organization.

By 1708, Mr. Street was physically unable to continue as pastor of the church, so after some negotiation and the promise of specific amounts of wheat, rye, Indian corn, pork and such firewood as was needed "over and above that received gratis," the granting of certain acreage for farming and pasture, and a new house, Rev. Samuel Whittelsey was installed in May 1710 as colleague to Mr. Street. He was a graduate of Yale, 1705, and a fellow of Yale College but he offset these deficiencies in part by marrying the granddaughter of President Chauncey of Harvard College. Mr.

Whittelsey continued as pastor for 42 years until his death on Aug. 18, 1752. He was one of the most eminent preachers and distinguished men of his time.

Before his death Mr. Whittelsey had sensed a latent strife and division in his congregation which was actually a reflection of the ferment in both civil and political circles. The people were unable to agree on any candidate so a committee was appointed to try to settle the matter. Wisely as it seemed at the time they wrote to President Holyoke of Harvard to suggest a candidate and he came forward with Mr. James Dana of the Harvard Class of 1753 and only 23 years old. Having preached and been approved he was given the call and accepted.

However, doubt soon arose among some members as to whether his doctrine was sound with regard to original sin, the saints' perseverance, free will and falling from grace. Apparently Mr. Dana was an early example of the genus Harvard of whom it is said "You can always tell a Harvard man, but you can't tell him much" because he replied to inquiries on these important matters flippantly and in "a loud and boisterous manner."

Such disrespect for his elders and levity in a position which demanded a serious and solemn demeanor gave rise to a solid body of opposition in the church which crystallized into the great controversy between the Old Lights and the New Lights. This opened a new era in New England theology and the "liberties of the churches."

In brief, the confrontation was whether the Congregational Church in Wallingford could install Mr. Dana in the face of the opposition of a substantial body of its own parishioners plus that of the consociation New Haven County. The two opposing groups met in Wallingford on the same day, Oct. 10, 1758. Long resolutions were voted, but there is no record of fisticuffs.

The controversy continued over several years and

in 1762 reached a crisis when the opposition to Mr.
Dana left the church, called a new minister and formed
the Wells Society. This was followed by injunctions and
other legal actions, but finally in 1787, unable to
support Mr. Waterman any longer, the Wells group
reunited with the Congregational Church, by that time
under the pastorate of Rev. James Noyes.

The controversy historically marked the end of the
rigid control of both civil and ecclesiastical affairs by
the church elders. Mr. Dana brought to Connecticut the
liberal theological views which had been promulgated in
the Boston area and which ultimately gave birth to
Unitarianism. In later years as a leading spirit in
fomenting the Revolution he became very popular, and
as a theologian received the degree of Doctor of Divinity
from the University of Edinburgh.

In 1785 his poor health necessitated the
appointment of a colleague, Mr. James Noyes, but a few
years later, his health restored, he became the pastor of
the First Church in New Haven, one of the most
prestigious in New England. The undaunted spirit of the
man is shown by the fact that in 1805, at the age of 70,
he was deeply wounded when asked to "retire from his
pastoral duties." As late as April 1, 1812, he was active
in the affairs of the church, and died in August, 1812, at
77. President Dwight of Yale preached the funeral
sermon.

There is no question that Mr. Dana was one of the
most illustrious men of his era and a leader in shaking
off the shackles of the past in both the ecclesiastical and
governmental circles of society, and while Wallingford
cannot claim the honor of his birth, it was here that he
accomplished his most effective work.

CHAPTER 10

Return Jonathan Meigs

One October evening in 1739, a young man stormed angrily out of a house in Middletown. He had just been rejected for the third time by a pretty Quaker girl, and had informed her in no uncertain terms that he, Jonathan Meigs, was through for good and she would see him no more. Just as he was about to mount his horse, the door opened and a voice came through the darkness, "Return, Jonathan, Return, Jonathan, Won't thou please return, Jonathan?"

Jonathan went back and on Dec. 17, 1740, a son was born. "Thou will have the naming of the boy, Jonathan," said his wife. And added wistfully, "I hope you choose Jonathan." "Aye, he will be Jonathan," said his father, "but I have another idea. The sweetest words I ever heard were "Return Jonathan" and that is what he shall be named."

To the great distress of his parents, young Jonathan grew up into an unruly and lawless man who was caught passing counterfeit money in New York, jailed, tried, convicted and sentenced to be hanged. However, his father was a man of influence and the Governor, Council and General Assembly of Connecticut petitioned the Governor of New York, and he was pardoned. This experience served to dampen, temporarily at least, this bold adventurer, or at least to direct his energies into more normal channels for in 1775 he was in business in Middletown and captain of a militia company.

When news of Lexington arrived, he led his company to Cambridge, and so distinguished himself at the siege of Boston that he was assigned as a commander under Arnold in his expedition against Quebec. His journal of this famous march, the attack on Quebec, his capture and exchange, all written by mixing powder and water in his hand, is available in Kenneth Robert's "March to Quebec."

After his exchange, Meigs returned to the army with the rank of Lieutenant Colonel, and was assigned to Connecticut troops. In the spring of 1777, the British sent out a large foraging party to Sag Harbor on the eastern tip of Long Island. Word of this movement was sent to Connecticut and Meigs seized the opportunity to strike, though to the observer the circumstances seemed to offer difficulties beyond successful solution.

In brief, Meigs loaded 160 men in whaleboats at Sachem's Head and under convoy of two armed sloops and an extra sloop to bring back prisoners — rowed across Long Island Sound, reached Sag Harbor at 2 a.m. captured the entire British party of 90 men, burned 12 transports and the collected forage, and returned to Guilford at noon without the loss of a man, having rowed a hundred miles in 18 hours. For this feat, certainly the most extraordinary of the Revolution, Meigs was thanked by Congress and awarded a sword.

In Guilford at the time lived the Scranton family, one of whose sons was to found Scranton, Pa. But more interesting was a bevy of seven daughters whose names conjure up a strange melange of ideas — Charity, Content, Freelove, Joy, Mercy, Mindwell and Submit. Indeed with such attractions right at home it is passing strange that Meigs got his expedition off at all. Possibly the explanation is that in that era, our culture had not' reached the stage when young ladies sing, "Come help yourself to my lips, etc." If it had, there would be only one guess necessary as to which young lady would have been most popular with Meigs' 160 men!

And this leads to further question. In our

egalitarian society it comes as a shattering blow to our social concepts of what that society should be that this song so popular among our young people should use the singular. Why should any individual have such special privileges? This is gross discrimination of race, creed, color or sex (ah, there's the discrimination), and smacks of capitalistic exploitation. I demand that the song henceforth be rendered "Come help yourselves" to presumably anything you want! I hope this digression will be excused for when my emotions are deeply aroused, I lose my judgment and perspective, and, in fact, feel young again.

If by this time you haven't forgotten all about Colonel Meigs, you will be interested to know that as colonel of the Leather Cap regiment he stormed Stony Point with General "Mad" Anthony Wayne, and took over command of West Point after Arnold's treason. After his retirement in 1781, he became surveyor for the Ohio Company, and later U.S. Indian Agent to the Cherokees. At 82, he gave up his quarters to an elderly Indian Chief, moved to a tent, contracted pneumonia and died on Jan. 28, 1823.

Return Jonathan Meigs' son became Governor of Ohio and Postmaster General, and indeed the whole family has been one of great distinction. The name to us in Wallingford is most familiar in the context of the Meigs Point section of Hammonasset Beach. The purchase of that magnificent stretch of beach from the Indians is recorded on a doe skin where the price is duly set down as one jug of rum and a hunting knife.

Recently the Meigs family group made a gift of $400,000 to Wesleyan University to endow a chair in American history in honor of Return Jonathan Meigs.

CHAPTER 11

Wharton Brook

If it were not for Wharton Brook State Park, the little stream which gave the park its name would probably be unknown to the dwellers in Ridgeland and the other farflung environs of Wallingford, but to the small boy of the 1890's this brook which meanders from its source in the broad flatlands of North Farms down through the center of town to the State Park and then on through the sand plains to the Quinnipiac was a veritable paradise for exploration and adventure.

From its beginnings the brook trickles into Frank Hill's ice pond, a favorite swimming place for both town boys and those Choaties who found their way there by day, and, I must say, by night. For us small boys, it was too far from town on a hot day and too dangerous, so we waited for the water farther down stream after it flowed through the little valley, down the bottom of a long ravine, into Campbell's pond, and eventually down through the fields to Simpson's.

The stretch of ravine north of Campbell's, hedged in by high steep rocky banks and deeply shaded by huge oaks, pines and hemlocks was an ideal place for boys to carry on Indian fighting, camping, paddling, and all the boisterous activities of youth. Despite surrounding housing developments this ravine, by its innate intransigence, has remained impregnable to the encroachments of civilization and retains its pristine wilderness character.

However, it is about the various swimming holes along Wharton's Brook that I should like to comment. Although we played all about Campbell's pond, I do not remember ever swimming in it, but as the brook emerged into the meadows, it broadened out into a lovely pool just above the bridge where Christian Street crossed it.

It was to this pool that a group of us boys including the late John W. Leavenworth, later famous as halfback on the Yale 1905 football team when only thirteen men played the full sixty minutes against Princeton and Harvard, was walking out Christian Street one hot summer day when, as we came over the brow of the hill, John gave a wild whoop, leaped the fence into the field, and started racing down toward the brook. The reason was obvious. There outlined against the green alders was a slim white naked body with long chestnut curls tumbling over the shoulders. The excitement was quickly quenched when closer inspection revealed Maurice Milcke whose father, the concert violinist, was grooming him in the European tradition as a boy prodigy.

The next popular swimming spot along the brook was Simpson's pond, where on one July 4th night after the bon-fire under an old apple tree on the west bank I first swam. I believe there was another "hole" at the north end where the brook entered the pond.

I suppose no fish could or would live in Wharton's Brook today, and indeed trout had disappeared when I was a boy. There were suckers which we used to spear by torchlight up above Campbell's, and my brother and I snared about twenty-four pounds of pickerel in the pool below Simpson's dam after a torrential Autumn rain.

Worth noting also is the confluence of Gunpowder Creek north of the Center Street bridge. This tiny stream, named after the Atwater gunpowder factory which provided ammunition for Washington's Army, flows down through the Choate campus. In the days

when the Quinnipiac Indians hunted in Wallingford this
whole valley was a morass of brush and alders called by
the Indians Bear Swamp.

There may well have been other pools frequented
by neighborhood boys between Simpson's and the
wooden bridge where South Elm Street crossed over to
Pond Hill, but if so I never used them. However, this
hole was a favorite, and it was there one day, when we
were romping around, naked as usual, that a barouche,
drawn by a pair of high steppers and containing besides
the coachman Mrs. C. H. Tibbits and her mother, Mrs.
Gurdon Hull, was heard approaching. We boys
scrambled to get under the bridge where we were well
showered with dirt, sand and gravel coming through the
cracks as the equipage rattled over the planks.

I have no doubt other pools existed south of town
though, of course, the present large one at the State
Park is new. There is no doubt, however, that the
swimming hole par excellence of the town was at
Ginty's Spring where one of the channels of the
Quinnipiac makes a wide sweep to the East before
flowing into Community Lake. Here oaks and beeches
spread their branches out over the water so a boy could
swing out and drop off into the deep water of the river.

I never went swimming at Ginty's nor did any of
my companions for good and sufficient reasons.
Nowhere is zenophobia exhibited in more virulent form
than between gangs of boys, and we had no stomach to
invade this sacred retreat of the belligerent and hard
fisted Irish boys. Even today the place is lovely and
serene. Hopefully, Wallingford will eventually overcome
its inertia and acquire the wastelands along the river for
public recreation in accordance with the fully
documented survey made some years ago by my son,
Peter Hale.

The allure of the old swimming holes, now silted
and overgrown, can never be replaced by the public and
many private pools, but perhaps it is not too much to
look forward to the time when, with pollution

eliminated, Ginty's Spring may resound with the shouts of boys and bring to life again the charm and flavor of a century long gone.

CHAPTER 12

The Seething Pot

The period from 1762 to 1775 following the French and Indian War was one of political ferment in Wallingford and throughout New England. The troubled times of the preceding years had resulted in a feeling of unity and strength among the colonists generally. This was soon tested by attempts on the part of England to bring this growing off-spring to heel by regulations on trade and administration, and financially by imposition of taxes such as the Stamp Act of 1763. This laid a tax on every skin, piece of vellum, or parchment, or sheet or piece of paper "for all legal documents, covering almost all transactions between men." This was compounded by passage of the "Sugar Bill" which laid a duty on various luxury items.

Growing indignation spread through the colonies and a Wallingford town meeting of 1766 enunciated the doctrine of "born free" and levied a fine of 20 shillings on any person using stamped paper. The Stamp Act was repealed but it was followed by other oppressive statutes of a kindred nature. England with its usual stubbornness was determined to bring about the subjection of the colonies. This effort culminated in the Boston Port Bill, the result of which was to destroy all trade in Boston. This was too much. A town meeting voted to solicit subscriptions for the relief of Boston, and in 1774 preparations were made to raise militia for defense.

From the January 13th of 1766 when the Sons of Liberty rode through the town calling upon all to resist the Stamp tax until Wallingford men left for Boston after the news came of Lexington and Concord, the town joined in the growth of the revolutionary spirit.

Public opinion was not by all means unanimous. As was to be expected, many people clung to their allegiance to the throne of England, and regarded the resistance as both treasonable and foolish. These so called "Tories," while in the minority, were generally men of substance and influence. Nevertheless they were submerged in the fervor of the patriots and many left for havens like Nova Scotia which is filled with New England names today, while others were imprisoned.

Wallingford had its share of Tories, but the most famous was not a local person. He was William Franklin, natural son of Benjamin Franklin. Having been proclaimed in New Jersey "a virulent enemy of the colonies" he was exiled to Wallingford where he was held under arrest at the Carrington house, a fine large colonial structure which stood during my boyhood on the present site of the Masonic temple. In the garden behind the house with its boxwood paths, Franklin received callers, and doubtless carried on his "Toryism," since he stayed here only a few months, was transferred to Middletown, and thence to the Litchfield jail where he was eventually confined without pen, ink or paper.

Wallingford did its full share in the Revolutionary War in providing men, munitions and stores. The Atwater powder mill on the small creek that runs through the Choate School fields provided ammunition for Washington's Army. The complete historical details of the men who served, the battles in which they were engaged, and the labors and anxieties of the women on the home front are all available to those interested. It is enough to mention here that Wallingford men fought and died in almost all the great battles of the Revolution including Bunker Hill, the Brandywine, Saratoga, Bennington and Valley Forge.

Wallingford men went with Benedict Arnold on his expedition up the Kennebec River and through the wilds of Maine, suffering almost unsufferable hardships, to the walls of Quebec. Lieutenant John Mansfield in October, 1781, led the "forlorn hope" storming party over the redoubt at Yorktown, the capture of which broke the back of the British resistance, and led to the surrender of Cornwallis. Wallingford has never been invaded by an enemy but the margin has been narrow. In 1779 General Tryon led an expeditionary force up the sound and dropped anchor in New Haven harbor about midnight on July 4th. The following morning Captain Abraham Stanley marched his Company to New Haven and participated in the defense of the city, a defense in which President Stiles of Yale was prominent. The same company participated in the action at Fairfield, and men from Wallingford also fought in the raid on Danbury.

Some estimates of the whole-hearted engagement in the Revolution by the men of Wallingford can be made from the list of officers headed by Colonel Street Hall and including two majors, twenty five captains, thirteen lieutenants and five ensigns. The number of men serving at various times runs into the hundreds. Notable among the men from Wallingford who fought in the Revolution were two slaves, Chatham Freeman and another registered only as "Black Boss." Slavery in Connecticut was a gentle institution and often resulted in strong ties of affection, so it is probable that these two accompanied their masters to war as full fledged volunteers.

CHAPTER 13

Aaron Burr

Early on the morning of a beautiful autumn day in the year 1773 a horseman cantered briskly up So. Main St., raising an appreciative eye now and then to the substantial residences lining the street and no less to those young women busy with window or porch, rounded the corner into Center St. and drew up before the tavern.

Dismounting and tying his horse to the post, he entered the tap room to find Master Carrington occupied shining glasses and making ready for the day's trade.

"I am Aaron Burr of Princeton," he introduced himself. "Has my uncle, Mr. Edwards, been in this morning?"

"Hain't seen him yet," replied Carrington, "but he most generally drops in when he is aroun' town."

Burr was a slender, alert youth of 17 with a quick nervous manner of speech and action.

"He's due to meet me here this morning, and conduct me to his new plantation, but doubtless I am somewhat early."

Footsteps sounded from the hall, and a tall, broad-shouldered young man of some 23 years advanced quickly and held out his hand.

"Aaron, my boy, am I happy to see you!" Then looking Burr over from head to toe, he remarked, "Boy no longer, but then I haven't seen you for two years.

You've been too busy with your studies to come so far."

"Too true, Uncle Pierpont," said Aaron. "When father established the college his first rule was 'No fighting, no gaming, no drinking or dicing.' Fortunately, he didn't forbid wenching and cock fighting so we do have some amusements. To tell the truth, though, I have studied hard, especially the past year since I was graduated."

"It's early for a libation, so let's start home where I can refresh you with a glass of my Madeira."

The two mounted and rode at a leisurely pace clattering over the rattling bridge at Wharton's Brook and then up the series of hills to the East Durham Rd. At the top they stopped to breathe their horses and turned to view the countryside behind. In every direction was a mass of green forest from which rose the sharply cut hills to the northwest and the rolling masses of the Sleeping Giant to the southwest.

Shortly beyond the crest of the hills, Edwards turned to the right off the Durham road into a lane which led over the breast of a hill through a row of large maples. Heavy woods bordered the south side where the land sloped upward, but on the left some fields had been cleared and were planted to corn, oats, buckwheat and other crops. Amidst the corn the pumpkins shone in the brilliant sun like huge globes of gold.

They soon came to a gate and before them stood the house, wide, ample and friendly, welcoming them as it basked in the warm September sun. Edwards regarded the scene with obvious pride and said:

"It's going to take time to develop the gardens properly, clear those woods to the east, and do some further landscaping, but it's a good start, I think, for this short time."

A high, two-wheeled cart filled with sacks appeared from back of the house, and the two drew aside to let it pass.

"That's corn going down the road to Tyler's mill to

be ground," commented Edwards. "And by the way, the stream that turns the mill is just over yonder hill. If you will stay awhile you can fill your creel in half an hour with as fine trout as you can find anywhere. It's rarely fished, as the boys in town catch all they want in the river or Wharton's brook. Oh, I almost forgot," he continued, "keep a sharp lookout for copperheads. The ridges are full of them, and sometimes they get down to the brook."

At the door they were welcomed by Mrs. Edwards and two little girls, one their daughter with fair complexion and chestnut hair, the other a dark creamy brown with her hair in two tight pig-tails.

Mrs. Edwards kissed Aaron and said; "Here is Susan; no longer the baby when you saw her last, and this is her playmate, Flora." Both girls made a deep curtsy and then ran off giggling down the garden path. Edwards looked after them fondly and said: "We found Susan was very lonesome here with no playmates conveniently near, so we were lucky to find Flora. I bought her from a Mr. Isaac Hale of Glastonbury. He was loath to part with her, but when I explained the situation and begged him to let me have her for Susan, he finally acquiesced at a good stiff price. But it's worth it to see them both so happy."

Soon after, the men sat enjoying a glass of Madeira in the library.

"An excellent wine," commented Aaron with all the assurance of a connoisseur.

His uncle smiled with amusement.

"You do me honor, Aaron," he replied. "I was so fortunate as to procure several pipes in New Haven from a shipmaster I know who brought it directly from the Island."

"But tell me, Aaron," he continued, "what have you been doing and what are your plans?"

"Well, sir," Aaron settled back in his chair, "after I was graduated from Princeton last year, I was only 16, so I decided to spend a year completing my education there. Grinding at Greek and Latin and experimenting in the natural sciences don't leave much time for reading history, political science, or the English classics, and learning something of music and the arts. Certainly without these no one can be considered an educated man."

"With that I agree completely," nodded Edwards

"Yes, I agree that the study of Greek and Latin is not the end-all of education, but it should be the foundation. The grind may be tedious, but it puts a lasting polish on the mind, and mastering a dull and difficult task teaches it to concentrate and to bring all your faculties to bear on the duty in hand, no matter how difficult and irksome. The mind, like the body, must be exercised, trained, disciplined and stretched to the full extent of its capacity. Education is not what you learn so much as developing your intellectual powers. Besides," he concluded with a sly glance, "there is nothing more effective in court room or public oration than an apt quotation from the classics especially if no one knows its meaning."

"But, sir, I am not headed for the law. I have decided to follow in the footsteps of my father and grandfather in the ministry."

"They wore large shoes," commented Edwards, "especially your grandfather — and that is not any derogation of your father. Jonathan Edwards was a powerful preacher against sin, and hell-fire and damnation were powerful deterrents."

"I'm afraid they are not my forte," said Aaron quietly. "I am on my way to Bethlehem to study theology with Dr. Bellamy."

"Ah, there's a horse of a different color," exclaimed Edwards. "A very sound man in a quiet way. I liked what he said that when he was young he thought it was the thunder that killed, but when he learned it was the lightning, he decided to thunder less and lighten more."

Both men laughed and after a brief silence,
Edwards asked:

"How was your journey? Pleasant, I hope."

"Yes, indeed. Fortunately, the weather was good. I
lay last night at New Haven so I had an opportunity to
see the college. The students seemed to me a motley
group, lounging on the fence in front of Connecticut
Hall, quite different in bearing and quality from my
friends at Princeton."

His uncle started up in mock horror.

"Would you defame — would you cast aspersion —
on the institution your own father honored with his
presence? One would think from your bias you had
been graduated from the infamous halls of Harvard."

"Oh, Uncle Pierpont, I criticize not the institution
but the rabble. After all, why would father have started
the college at Princeton except to improve over Yale?
At least neither is infected by the atheistic doctrines
prevalent at Cambridge!"

At that moment the deep baying of hounds came
through the open windows.

"Those damned dogs," exploded Edwards,
"they're down in Tamarack again."

With that he rushed out of the house with Aaron in
close pursuit.

"Zeke," yelled Edwards, "Zeke, where are you?"

"Here I is, Boss," came a shout from the barn, "I
was just agoin' after 'em."

"What's the trouble, Uncle?" asked Aaron.

Edwards pointed with his hand to a tangled mass
of live and dead trees, covered with vines that extended
along the base of the ridges to the east.

"That's Tamarack, the worst swamp anywhere
around here. It's full of raccoons, wild cats, foxes, the
Lord knows what, and even bear have been seen. The
bog is so soft and deep that a man can disappear in the
mire like a stone in water. Of course, the dogs are
possessed to get in there, and all too often one or two of
my best ones don't come out."

"While we're out here, Aaron," continued his uncle, "come see my pistol alley."

They walked toward a corner of the gardens where a rectangular plot of level ground had been carefully laid out surrounded by a cedar hedge. At one end a post in the figure of a man facing sideways was erected.

Edwards became deadly serious.

"In these days, there are so many rascals in public life it's necessary to be constantly on guard to protect one's honor and," with a sidelong glance at Aaron, "the best protection I know is to have a reputation as a dead shot. Wait a moment while I fetch my pistols."

Soon he returned with a case which he opened to reveal two long barreled pistols with ivory handles. "I bought these in Paris. They are the finest I have ever seen. Take one — it isn't loaded — and go to that marker and turn your back on the post. Now as I count you walk seven paces — one, two, three, four, five, six, seven — Present! At that word you turn, take aim and fire at the post. But wait! I am going to make you privy to my secret. Never fire your pistol at the word 'present.' Continue counting in your mind — eight, nine, ten."

"But why give that advantage?" asked Aaron.

"Because most of the men you meet are inexperienced and nervous. At the word 'present' they turn quickly and with a shaking hand the chances of their hitting you are relatively small. On the other hand, if you take the extra three seconds, you have time to steady your hand and aim carefully. Also you have the moral satisfaction of being attacked first."

Edwards loaded a pistol, and under his instruction Aaron made several practice shots.

"Do this every day while you're here, and you should become reasonably proficient."

During his stay, Aaron spent the time fishing and shooting, so when a few days later he waved goodbye gaily to the group on the porch and galloped off down the lane on his way to Litchfield, he was prepared to meet his destiny.

In this sketch, I have mingled fact and fantasy. History records that Aaron Burr did visit his Uncle, Judge Pierpont Edwards, at his plantation on Tamarack Road. The curious can see just beyond the culvert on the east side of the road the outlines of a foundation and cellar, and, by pushing aside an inch or two of soil, the cellar wall of a large house, still remembered by local residents. There as one looks over the rolling meadows to the Totoket hills the lovely landscape provides the visual reason for the selection of the site by Judge Edwards.

The characters are real. Judge Edwards maintained close relations with Burr and acted as his political lieutenant in Connecticut. I have the conveyance by which my great, great, great grandfather, Timothy Hale, sold Flora, then five years old, to his son Isaac for fifteen pounds, though I am responsible for her coming to Wallingford.

Finally, it is recounted that in Burr's famous duel with Hamilton, at the command "Present," Hamilton fired at once and missed, while Burr waited two or three seconds to fire the fatal shot.

CHAPTER 14

George Washington Didn't Sleep Here

On the beautiful morning of June 29, 1775, His Excellency General George Washington, newly appointed Commander of the Continental Army, rode up So. Main St., turned into Center St. and stopped in front of the inn. With him were his aides, Major General Charles Lee, Major Thomas Missin and Samuel Griffin. The party was on its way to Cambridge, where Washington was to take command of the army.

It was near noon so word went out quickly to the town officials and clergy to gather at the tavern to dine with General Washington. Since he was an Episcopalian, it was deemed fit that the Rev. Mr. Andrews offer thanks; although it was rumored that he in common with many Church of England ministers had Tory sympathies. The Rev. Mr. Waterman of the Wells Society in asking blessings on all and sundry became so voluble that fiery Charles Lee sat down abruptly and began to eat.

Rev. Andrews in asking the blessing upon the conclusion of the meal took the occasion to rebuke Mr. Waterman – apparently the two divines were not on too good terms – by inserting in his remarks the following passage from the Bible: "Be not rash with thy mouth and let not thine heart be hasty to utter anything before God: for God is in Heaven and thou upon earth; therefore, let thy words be few." If not greeted by unseemly applause, this sally probably provoked some sly smiles, and we can imagine a brief flicker even crossed Washington's stern mouth.

It is perhaps not always realized that Washington was only 43 years old when appointed Commander-in-Chief of the Army, and thus had placed on his shoulders the destiny of the United States and ultimately those of the political world. Rarely does history focus so bright a light on an individual and especially one so young. Fortunately, the shoulders were broad to withstand the rigors and strains of the years to follow.

Washington was richly endowed by nature. He was six feet three and one-half inches tall and without an ounce of surplus flesh weighed about 200 pounds. His muscular strength was proverbial. Two men were required to lift his large wartime tent and poles, but Washington with one hand raised them and threw them into the baggage cart. This then was the young man who stayed in Wallingford for an hour or two in those crucial times of the nation's history.

Fourteen years later, early on the morning of Oct. 19, 1789, a great traveling coach white in color and drawn by four horses with postillions and out-riders and a large retinue in uniforms drew up before the inn of Master Jeremiah Carrington which was situated where the east end of the Municipal Building now stands. We are told that Washington arrived unexpectedly, though that seems hardly possible even in those days since the party had spent the previous two nights and all of Sunday in New Haven. There can be no doubt, however, that Master Carrington was thrown into a tizzy to have a party of several dozen men including the President of the United States drop in for breakfast and it is no wonder that as a result Washington recorded in his diary for posterity that "Carrington's is but an ordinary house" in so doing drawing sharp contrast with Mr. Brown's in New Haven who he notes "keeps a good tavern." Indeed, it is doubtful that Master Carrington if he had been aware of these entries would have promptly upon Washington's departure renamed his place of business "The Washington Inn." Anyway, Washington stopped, even if he didn't sleep, there.

The purpose of this journey through New England was to familiarize the President with the resources of the country, agricultural, manufacturing and mercantile. In these days the ulterior purpose would be to estimate how much in taxes could be levied, and no doubt since Washington was a practical man and had the responsibility of a new government to support, something of the same nature could have been in his mind.

Washington's diaries, however dull for casual reading, take on immense interest historically because of the meticulous care with which he set down his observations. On his stay in New Haven he comments that "New Haven is said to number about 9000 souls; also has an Episcopal Church, 3 Congregational meeting houses and a college." Why Washington chose to record this almost insulting anonymity must be left to some Harvard aspirant for a Ph.D in history! It is interesting to note that while in New Haven Washington dined with Pierpont Edwards, already mentioned as a Wallingford resident, Governor Huntington, Lieut. Governor Wolcott and Mayor Roger Sherman.

According to his diary, Washington after spending Sunday in New Haven set out at 6 a.m. on his journey to Wallingford. Passing through East Haven he comments about the "extensive marshes covered with hay stacks, a very pleasant ride along the river," but "the road is sandy and continues to be within a mile of the town. This is all the sand we have met with on the journey. These sandy lands afford but ordinary crops of corn."

Washington's comments about our sand plains bring back memories of the 90's when the present Route 5 was nothing but a cart track through the deep sand. A bicycle rider could make no progress through it at all, so in order to reach Toelle's Rest and a glass of cool beer, the Wallingford Cycle Club constructed a path of crushed rock beside the road. Along this the sports of the 90's pedalled at a furious 15 miles an hour, led by John Cottrill, bent over the low slung handle bar in a horizontal position.

The Washington party emerged from the sand on to the firm ground of Parsons St. and arrived at Carrington's at 8:30 for the breakfast already described. After breakfast the General took a stroll through the town and noted white mulberry trees being grown, and examined silk worms and cocoons and the resultant silk woven into lustring, a heavy glossy fabric, and silk thread. Today there are still mulberry trees scattered around town, but the silk industry has disappeared.

Long tradition has it that as Washington took his after breakfast walk about town, which as he describes it "stands upon high and pleasant ground," he stopped to rest, as it may have been a very hot day, under the large elm tree in front of the Royce house on the corner of Main and North Streets. Certainly, this enormous elm, probably the oldest tree in town, planted perhaps by Nehemiah himself about 1671, was always called the "Washington Elm."

It had a circumference of about 20 feet and a spread of 110 feet. When I was a boy it was fun for several of us to stow ourselves away in a large hole at the base. It was blown down in 1896, but Henrik Hillbom painted several pictures of it, one of which is on view at the Royce house, and another at the Historical Society. Also several pieces of the elm have been preserved and are among the historical objects in the Royce house.

While I dislike to assume the role of an iconoclast with regard to an ancient and honored tradition, I submit as facts that Washington states in his diary he arrived in Wallingford at 8:30 a.m. and left about 10 a.m. During this 90-minute period he records breakfasting — and remember, no preparations had been made previously to provide for him and his retinue strolling around town, and examining into the silk industry. His stroll must have been constantly interrupted by greetings and conversations with the people. I must confess that I find it improbable that any man under the circumstances described could have breakfasted, greeted the townspeople, discussed the silk and probably other industry of the town, walked the nearly two miles to North St. and back, all in about 90 minutes, and all without including any record of his following Franklin's sage advice and visiting the necessary before departure.

The route Washington took to Durham has been much disputed. It seems reasonably certain he left Carrington's Inn, now marked by a metal shield opposite Fair St., proceeded east to the present McKenzie Reservoir, then north to junction of Scard Rd. and Washington Trail, over the saddle of the hill to the road by Blue Trail Range, then to avoid the large swamp area, now mostly filled in by railroad and road, around the north side of Reed's Gap. If one stops on the Durham Rd. west of the new bridge, an old road is plainly visible between two lines of trees going north and bending around through the gap. Members of my family who lived on the spot for generations have testified to this route.

Beyond the gap the route swung sharply right behind Totoket Mountain — the quarry   and emerged on the New Haven to Middletown Rd. Some of this abandoned road is plainly visible where a Washington Trail marker, now almost totally obscured by undergrowth, has been placed on the' road North of Page's Corner where the old road emerges on Tri-Mountain Rd. The part of the road which ran into the New Haven - Middletown Rd. is still open and used and marked "Old Washington Trail." A rough trip but he made it and encountered only swamps instead of sand!

It is pleasant to think of this commanding and historic figure on the streets of Wallingford greeting the people and observing the life of the town. These brief visits of Washington to Wallingford do not seem so remote as to lose reality when one considers that if my own grandfather had been born in Wallingford instead of Glastonbury, he would as a small boy of eight doubtless have been among the urchins scampering about in the excitement, gazing with awe at the coach and uniforms, and perhaps even shaking the hand of the Father of his Country.

CHAPTER 15

A Romance of '76

This is a story of old Wallingford. It is based partly on historical fact, partly on tradition, and incidentally on fantasies which may indeed have been facts.

- - - - - - - -

One rainy afternoon when I was a boy my mother, to rid herself of my complaints about having nothing to do, suggested that I go down to Sally Carrington's house and perhaps with a couple of other playmates we could pass the time.

The Carrington House was on Center St. and was razed when the present Municipal Building was constructed. The house itself had been erected on the site of the old Carrington Tavern of Revolutionary times, of which Sally's great, great grandfather had been tavern keeper. Thus it was natural that the attic in Sally's house was a fascinating place for children since it held the keepsakes, mementos and furnishings of generations. I have forgotten the details of that afternoon's rummaging of old chests, dressing up in ancient hats and dresses and the childish excitement over discovered treasures except for a small packet of letters I found tucked away in an old chest.

To be frank, my interest was philatelic, a word I have acquired since as I have become more knowledgeable in my stamp collecting. Because I was curious why the letters had no stamps but were perhaps important by reason of having been kept so long, I decided to take them down to Mrs. Carrington. She untied the fading ribbon, saying, "yes, these are letters to Sally's great aunt. Leave them with me and I'll tell you about them later."

- - - - - - - -

Late on the afternoon of June 28, 1781, a small cavalcade rode into Wallingford from the East and dismounted at the Carrington tavern. All were in uniform, but only one wore the well known Continentals, so it was apparent the strangers were French. As Master Carrington greeted them at the door, the American advanced from the group and said,

"I am Colonel Burr of General Washington's staff. May I present the Duc de Lauzun and his staff. His men are camped East of here but the Duc prefers your accommodations for the night to his cot and army fare. Because I am familiar with this region – Judge Pierpont Edwards is my uncle – and with the French language, I am acting as guide and interpreter. You may remember I was here some years ago. We shall spend the night and leave at dawn. And, Master Carrington, our mission is secret and I must request strict privacy."

"My doors will be closed at once," replied Carrington. "I have no other guests. Dinner will be ready soon. Take your choice of rooms and make yourselves comfortable."

As the group assembled for dinner in the tap room, Master Carrington appeared at the door with a pretty, dark haired girl of 16. "Gentlemen," he said, "My daughter, Sally. She will serve you."

Colonel Burr glanced at the girl quizzically and then at one of the officers at the table, a handsome youth of perhaps 18 with blue eyes and the gold hair with reddish tints so characteristically French, tied in a single knot at the back of the neck. Addressing him in French, Burr said, "Chevalier, here is one to test your metal. New England's fairest against the aristocracy of France."

Then turning to Sally, he said smiling, "Let me introduce Chevalier Charles de Lameth, son of the Duc de Guise, who has generously come to join us in our war with England."

Sally swept down in a deep curtsy and the Chevalier advanced, bowed low and raised her hand to his lips.

After dinner, the officers gathered around the table, spread out papers and maps, and proceeded to discuss the campaign ahead. de Lameth, who was attached as an aide rather than an officer of the line, strolled out into the garden behind the inn. Suddenly, at a turn in the path he came upon Sally, sitting on a garden bench. Startled, she jumped to her feet with a little cry of surprise, but at once sat down again with a word about the loveliness of the evening. But how after nearly two centuries can we trespass on their merry but almost futile attempts at conversation in French and English, or guess what more subtle forms of communication took place during the long silences that intervened?

At dawn after a hasty breakfast the group left the tavern and mounted their horses. As they were about to leave, Sally ran out the door. Instantly de Lameth was off his horse and seized her hand, speaking rapidly in French. Puzzled, confused and blushing, she turned to Colonel Burr and asked, her lips quivering, "What does he say, Colonel Burr?"

"Charles is saying he admires you very much and is in fact greatly enamoured with you, and promises to return as soon as the war is over."

Sally gasped, covered her face with her hands in a gesture of amazement and modesty, and ran back into the tavern.

Then with swords and accouterments glancing in the morning sun and a clatter of hoofs, the cavalcade rode off on the road to New Haven, Dobbs Ferry and eventually Yorktown.

When I came down from the attic, Mrs. Carrington was rocking silently in her chair, the letters carefully tied up again in the ribbon, and she looked as if she had been crying.

"Where did you find these, Clarence?" she asked. I told her how I had been pushing things around in the old chest, looking for stamps, when suddenly a little drawer snapped open and there were the letters.

"There is an old tradition in the Carrington family," she said slowly, "that during the Revolution a group of Rochambeau's officers stopped one night at the tavern, and one of the young aides fell deeply in love with his daughter, Sally. Now these letters prove how true it was, and with them is this letter which I will read as well as I can."

"Dear Mademoiselle Carrington:

It is with the utmost regret and in deep grief that I inform you that my beloved aide, Chevalier Charles de Lameth, fell at the siege of Yorktown. His last words were of his love and devotion for you and his earnest request for pardon for his failure to keep his promise to return.

de Lauzun"

A tear rolled down her cheek.

"Would you mind putting these back as closely as you can to where you found them?" she asked. "I would feel better to let them stay where she put them." As she handed them to me a few flakes of rose petals fell from the packet and crumbled into dust in my hand.

— — — — — — — —

Research whether historical, genealogical, medical or scientific can be either an exciting occupation or a fascinating by-way in the pursuit of happiness. From some source, perhaps the circumstances described later, or some historical reference or merely tradition, there has been lurking in my mind a belief that General de Rochambeau's forces passed through Wallingford during the Revolution.

De Rochambeau landed at Newport in May 1781, and later that month met with Washington at the Webb House in Wethersfield to plan their campaign. Accordingly, in June the French Army left Newport to march to join Washington's forces at Dobbs Ferry on the Hudson.

After leaving Rhode Island and camping at Windham on the third day, the map shows a split with the main body of troops proceeding along the route through Bolton to Hartford. This route offered the prospect of more plentiful supplies for the troops, probably a less rugged terrain, and less risk of attack from Long Island Sound. In this connection, Governor Trumbull had issued a proclamation requesting that the French troops be greeted hospitably and not be overcharged for necessary supplies. (How well he knew his Yankees!)

The other route, marked in red on the original map, turns southwest from South Windham (the present Route 207) through Lebanon to Colchester thence over present Route 16 to Middletown. From there, the map follows the route through Durham and Middlefield to Wallingford.

It thus seems obvious and history so records that de Rochambeau like a good general took care to guard the flanks of his moving army. To the north there was no risk but to the south the British controlled Long Island Sound and were heavily garrisoned in and about New York. It was therefore quite possible for them to move up the Sound to New Haven or Saybrook and strike his army from the side while disorganized and split during the crossing of the Connecticut at Hartford, or while stretched in a thin line of march over the roads west to Darbury.

Accordingly, he dispatched the Duc de Lauzun with a very considerable force consisting of 300 mounted hussars and 300 light infantrymen along the southern route to protect his flank from any possible British incursion. It was this force that on June 25,

DOBBS FERRY - 1781

A manuscript map, possibly by Louis Alexandre Berthier, of the famous meeting between the Comte de Rochambeau and General Washington at the Hudson River on the famous march from Providence, Rhode Island to join with the American troops.

Beinecke Library of Rare Books, Yale University

1781, probably bivouaced in the eastern section of Wallingford. Just where this camp was is not known. About ten years ago, the Interstate Rochambeau Committee erected a historic marker on the triangle of the junction of East Center Street, Scard and Northford roads. The marker read:

In this vicinity
French troops under
De Lauzun
Enroute to Yorktown
Encamped during June 1781

and was one of many erected to mark the routes taken by de Rochambeau's forces through Connecticut and adjacent states. It is typical of the vicious vandalism of the scum which smears our society that this marker has been stolen or destroyed and only the post remains.

Of de Lauzun, little information is available. Apparently, he was a typical French aristocrat of his time, and he seems to have participated joyously in the scandalous life of the court of Louis the Sixteenth. Probably he went on to engage in the siege and surrender of Yorktown, which brought about the victorious end of the Revolution, and was among those Frenchmen, who, as Pompidou recently reminded us, constituted a majority of all the troops engaged in that greatest of American victories.

What a sight it must have been to see those 600 French soldiers in their brilliant uniforms and glittering accouterments passing over the roads of the quiet countryside and perhaps making camp in the pleasant meadow that bordered Muddy River, the site now covered by the waters of the MacKenzie Reservoir. On a bright day, as the wind raises the surface into ripples one can imagine the French hussars rising from the watery depths with their helmets and sabres flashing in the sparkling sun.

And who knows, perhaps in some old chest in attic or auction room is yet a packet of letters hidden away, or if not, then a faint and hardly discernible smell of rose petals may linger and the haunting ghost of a memory of a garden bathed in moonlight.

CHAPTER 16

The Wheels Start to Whir

In the years following the Revolution, the formation of the Republic of the United States, and the administrations of Washington, Adams and Jefferson, Wallingford like all New England began to hum with industrial activity. The successful conclusion of the war and relief from the shackles of English rule gave a tremendous psychological lift to the people which resulted in a burst of energy, a release of inventive genius and productive work.

At that time the Village of Wallingford consisted of Main St., East Center St. and Elm St. There was little west of Main St. except the cemetery at the bottom of the hill, and the Main St. lots extended in some instances at least as far as the present Colony St. Indeed when Moses Beach built his palatial home on Main St. half a century later, his orchards extended beyond the bottom of the hill at the rear, and Orchard St. was laid out through this part of his land, whence of course came the name. As I have already noted, I believe, the scenic ponds on the grounds of the Country Club south of East Center St. resulted from the removal of loam to enrich the sandy soil of his orchards.

As was the common practice of the times, the various trades set up shop in or adjacent to their homes, and the streets of the village became studded with small enterprises. William Ward, at the corner of Ward St. manufactured beaver hats. Across the street Charles

Yale had a tinsmith business, and on a third corner was a carpenter, Captain William Todd. In a shop beside his residence, the present Historical Society House, Caleb Thompson made carriages with a sideline of coffins. The present Clulee residence was the site of Augustus Hull's blacksmith shop.

Next door was the house of Harry Beadle, built in 1801, beautifully preserved and recently renovated to its original condition. Mr. Beadle ran a fanning mill, a device for cleaning grain by the action of sieves and an air blast. I have always had a sentimental attraction for the Beadle house since it was at Miss Beadle's rooming and boarding house my father went to live when he came to Wallingford in 1879.

On the lot where Dr. Fraknoi now has his residence and office was the house of Benjamin Foote who had a tannery and shoe shop behind it at the foot of the hill. Some of his products went via New Haven to the West Indies, and he thus became Wallingford's first exporter of finished goods to foreign lands. On the site of my birthplace at 38 So. Main St. — now the Post Office — Colonel Caleb Cook carried on a shoe manufacturing business in competition with Mr. Foote.

On the Post Office corner was Hiram Yale's shop, the first maker of Britannia Ware. There was another shoe shop at Main St. near present Curtis Ave. On Center St. the Carringtons made coffee mills, and Elisha Pomeroy's razor strops were peddled throughout New England. Peddlers also distributed the products of Lyman Cannon's tin shop on the south side of Center St. Beyond Wharton's Brook on the site of the old street car barn, now a laundry, Deacon Fenn had a carpenter shop. Later the business became Fenn and Wooding and was the predecessor of the present C. F. Wooding Co.

There were, of course, many other enterprises in Wallingford, weavers, masons, coopers, and of course farmers in the surrounding countryside. Captain Macock Ward had a shop with lathes, gear cutters, wire drawing and screw cutting facilities. Here was invented the cyclometer, which attached to the wheel of the carriage rang a bell at the end of every mile. He also made and repaired clocks, and his apprentices went on to New Haven and Hartford. Ward was typical of the Yankee genius which established New England industry, and his like still exist in many New England towns.

Among the town's products at various times have been paper, glass (the factory was on Wharton's Brook west of the Simpson, Hall, Miller factory on East Center St.), the Wilson Sewing Machine, for which was built the "Rubber Shop" which took over after the failure of Wilson, bolts, wooden screws, and doubtless many other articles.

In the century from 1800 to 1900, many of these products were sold by "Yankee Peddlers" who started out from Wallingford with horse and cart loaded with various articles and traveled the whole East Coast of the country. Amos Francis was a typical Yankee Peddler who about 1817 traveled in marketing of tableware manufactured by the Yale Brothers. His contract set forth that he was to provide horse, wagon and harness, and was to receive $30 per month, and $40 if he cleared a profit over cost and expenses. Above that he received one-half of the profits, perhaps the earliest example of profit sharing in our capitalistic society.

CHAPTER 17

New Connecticut

The original charter of Connecticut from the King granted a strip of land about 75 miles wide extending from the shores of Long Island Sound westward to the shores of the Pacific Ocean. Following the conclusion of the Revolution, Connecticut promptly laid claim to all this land. Naturally a howl of protests immediately arose from New York, Pennsylvania and other interests, so overwhelming as to cause Connecticut to admit that such a claim was indeed ridiculous.

Accordingly Connecticut conceded the bulk of this vast territory to Congress as public land, but it was successful in reserving for Connecticut citizens a large chunk of land in what is now Northern Ohio. Its boundaries ran 120 miles West from Pennsylvania to the vicinity of the present city of Sandusky, along the shores of Lake Erie then down to a point south of present Youngstown. These lands were called "New Connecticut" or more commonly "The Western Reserve."

No sooner had this arrangement been effected than a group of energetic and far seeing men in Wallingford took steps to grasp this bonanza. The leader in the undertaking was Caleb Atwater, a man of great acumen and vigor, who had been active in manufacturing powder for the Revolutionary Army He lived in the "Red Cottage" on the present

Choate School grounds on Christian St. opposite the football field. He was a descendant of David Atwater, one of the founders of New Haven. Worth noting here is the amazing fecundity of this extraordinary family. In six generations it produced 114 families and 990 children. Individual families had children as follows: 1−15, 1−14, 4−13, 4−12, 7−11, 17−10, 23−8 and 16−6. Furthermore the Atwater beeed was outstanding in intelligence and physique, as I can attest from two brilliant school mates and a youthful sweetheart of unusual beauty.

It is to the Atwaters that Wallingford is indebted in that it is today the home of one of the finest preparatory schools in the nation, for Judge William Gardner Choate married Mary Atwater, the great-granddaughter of Caleb. She inherited the Atwater house on the corner of Christian and No. Elm streets, which the Choates used for many years as a summer home. (Yes, even in my time, New York families used to come to Wallingford for the summer).

In the 90's the Choates fostered Rosemary Hall, situated across the street on the northwest corner, but when that school removed to Greenwich, the Choates, who were childless, adopted the small tutoring school conducted by Dr. Mark Pitman, named it the Choate School, and thus started it on its career. Judge Choate was a prominent lawyer in New York, a brother of Joseph Choate, ambassador to Great Britain and the most famous wit of his time. During my New York years I used to dine beneath the portraits of these two distinguished men in the Harvard Club and their relationship to Wallingford used to give me a sense of homely satisfaction.

After adjusting with Congress and other interests its title to the Western Reserve, the Connecticut Assembly authorized a survey of this virgin territory totalling about 5260 square miles out of which eventually emerged ten Ohio counties plus other sections of the state. The Assembly then decided to put the land up for sale and settlement by Connecticut citizens, a sale conducted by a representative from every Connecticut county. The set price was 33 cents per acre which seems reasonable enough until one considers what inflation has done to the dollar in the meantime.

It is a highly interesting fact that the proceeds of this land sale were by vote of the Assembly deposited in a special fund to be used in support of the public schools of the state and this fund has contributed ever since to the education of Connecticut children.

Before the lands were sold, however, provision was made to except certain so called "Firelands" to be given to those who had suffered losses of their homes during the war from the British raids on New Haven, Fairfield, Danbury and other towns. Also Indian rights had to be purchased by the government and the Connecticut Land Company.

The enterprising and far-sighted group which seized upon the Western Reserve consisted of 48 men led by Caleb Atwater under the name of the Connecticut Land Company. This company promptly proceeded to buy all the remaining land in the Reserve and in 1796 sent out a party of men to make a complete survey. This and succeeding parties suffered great hardships both in making their way out to the Reserve, partly by overland routes and partly by way of the Great Lakes, and in running their lines through forests and swamps. Some of the men remained there over the winter, enduring further hardships, and were joined in the following year by others sent out from Connecticut.

In 1799 Caleb Atwater accompanied by Messrs. Merriman, Bunnell, Blakeslee and Hall went out to the Reserve to make an inspection of what had been accomplished and to formulate plans for the future settlement. General Moses Cleaveland was a leader in the survey and settlement, so it was natural that the site at the mouth of the Cuyahoga River selected for the principal projected city of the region should be named Cleveland. (Note the different spelling of the name.)

In 1800 Cleveland boasted three inhabitants. As a matter of fact the one acre city lots priced at $50 each found no buyers. Turhan Kirtland, the company agent, advised Mr. Atwater to "reduce the price or I shall never see it settled." Accordingly, the price was cut in half, and finally in desperation reduced to $12.50 per acre lot. At that the agent was empowered to take horses or cattle in payment, and even to sell on credit.

In the following years, settlement proceeded rapidly throughout the Reserve. Wallingford families moved out in substantial numbers – Cooks, Houghs, Doolittles, Upsons and Carringtons, Jones, Blakeslees and many other familiar names. Kirtland was one of the town's most favored, and it was here that Joseph Smith in 1833 built a Mormon Temple. Certain tenets of the Mormon faith, especially the polygamy practiced at that time, were a stench in the nostrils of these New Englanders, and eventually Smith and his followers were run out of town.

Caleb Atwater, as the prime entrepreneur in this great enterprise, took pains to see that he was not unrewarded in a material way. He owned and gave away thousands of acres including several whole townships. For instance, the town of Atwater he gave to his son Joshua, born in Wallingford in the "Red Cottage" in 1773, reserving 200 acres for religious purposes. Caleb also owned complete the town of Denmark and 5700 acres in Geneva. A tract of 6500 acres he owned in Auburn he split into 65 lots of 100 acres and gave one to each of his 55 grandchildren. Caleb had six daughters and one son. His descendants and those of other Wallingford settlers have been prominent in the professional, political and religious affairs of Ohio ever since.

The seed of these Connecticut families has spread

the Yankee traits and moral values throughout the West. The wide ranging and numerous family of Doolittles all stem from Abraham Doolittle of Wallingford. The old names come bobbing up everywhere. On television the other night appeared in Hollywood one Barry Atwater. A Barry Atwater went to school with me at Choate seventy years ago.

In the settlement of the West the contribution of Wallingford is unique. After the Revolution people poured West from the coastal states, over the Great Smokies, the Blue Ridge and the Alleghenies into the broad fertile plains of the Midwest. For the most part, this was a helter skelter migration of individual families from different communities. In the settlement of the Western Reserve, Wallingford particularly and Connecticut almost totally supplied the original population.

As a result, the towns, the churches, the architecture, the institutions, the religions and the people themselves were simply a transplantation from Connecticut, and even today it is probable this particular section of the country more closely resembles the Connecticut of a century and a half ago than does present Connecticut itself.

With good reason, Ohio University has as its motto, "The state has no material resources at all comparable with its citizens, and no hope of perpetuity except in the intelligence and integrity of its people."

Wallingford can indeed be proud of this chapter in her long history for these were and are Wallingford people.

CHAPTER 18

The Pekin Geese

A portrait I have of my grandfather reveals in the dour expression of his mouth and eyes a man not easily perturbed, and firm in his opinions. The former is confirmed by the fact that I have searched through his meticulously kept diaries of the years 1861-1865 for some mention of the Civil War, the assassination of Lincoln or even of his close friend, Gideon Welles, Secretary of War in Lincoln's cabinet, but without finding any reference whatsoever to men or events of this critical period in the history of the country.

That he was firm in his opinions is the burden of my story. Since it took place in Glastonbury, it is in a way disqualified from inclusion in these tales of old Wallingford, but since it certainly concerned me to an important degree that may be excuse enough for telling it. Anyway, I recount the story as it came to me piecemeal over the years in more or less subtle references during conversations between my father and grandmother. My grandfather's house was next to the Congregational Church, a fine old Colonial structure which still stands as uncompromisingly as ever on the main street of Glastonbury. Just as Wallingford had its bitter church controversy over the Old Lights and New Lights, so Glastonbury was not immune to the tides of change in religious doctrines, and this was made evident by the self-confident and rather bombastic young minister who came to Glastonbury about 1858 when my grandfather was already an old man of 77.

As grandfather listened on Sundays to sermons devoted to tearing down the authority and authenticity of the doctrines and credos of a lifetime as well as the exposition of youthful views on contemporary affairs which didn't exactly conform to grandfather's, his equanimity gave way to exasperation. The blowoff came in a vituperative sermon on slavery and slave owners, this being the hottest era of abolishionism. Slavery, my grandfather admitted, was outmoded, but he had fond memories of a kindly old man, his grandfather Timothy, who had been one of the largest slave owners in Connecticut, and he allowed also that George Washington was not the cruel, vengeful, lecherous character as all slave owners were depicted by the minister.

After that grandfather refused to go to church and have to listen to the "loud mouthed bellowing and damned nonsense," as he expressed it, of the minister. However, his irritation was only exacerbated by the fact that on Sunday mornings when the church windows were .open, and my grandfather was sitting on his back porch, he could not help hearing the stentorian tones of the preacher as they boomed out the windows and filled the air with more of the same fallacious dicta which had driven grandfather out of church. To a man of grandfather's character, this was an affront and situation which irked him to the marrow.

So, one winter evening, as he sat reading Gibbon's "Decline and Fall of the Roman Empire," one of his favorites in its classical background and the grandeur of its pessimism, he suddenly slapped his hand down on his knee and if he had had any knowledge of Greek would doubtless have shouted "Eureka" and startled his wife no end. As a thoughtful husband, he said nothing to his wife but the episode recorded by Gibbons of the sleeping Roman guards being awakened by the shrill cackling of the geese had in a flash given him the solution to his problem.

He lost no time in planning his strategic campaign for the approaching spring. A few weeks later a crate was delivered containing some large and strange looking specimens of the fowl family. "What on earth are those birds, Fraray?" enquired my grandmother who was no stranger to a barn yard. "Them's Pekin geese," briefly answered grandfather. "What do you want them for? Do they lay good?" asked my grandmother whose special perquisite was the egg money.

"I don't know and don't care. They'll dress up the place and be company for the other critters," affirmed grandfather.

"They'll keep us awake doing it," asserted grandmother as the geese by that time were creating bedlam among the chickens, the dog, and even the cows.

With that and having that rare wifely quality of avoiding fruitless argument — arguments with grandfather, I judge, were apt to prove fruitless — she went in the house. Grandfather promptly proceeded to construct a coop and wire enclosure for the geese on the south side of the barn which happened to be adjacent to the windows in the church nearest the pulpit.

The average person today has no contact with geese, especially the rare Pekin variety, but let it be said that geese can raise an awful ruction, and this breed has a particularly ear-splitting squawk. Even a casual conversation between gander and flock is usually enough to drown out ordinary noise, and let something occur to arouse the suspicions of the geese that all is not well and the volume rises to a shattering explosion of sound.

As grandfather had hoped rather than perhaps expected, the moment the reverend began his sermon one lovely morning in the spring with the church windows open and his voice came ringing out in stentorian tones, the geese, possibly egged on by a stone thrown against the coop, took immediate alarm and set up a horrendous gabbling. It was really no contest. Soon after service, the minister came storming into grandfather's yard and minced no words.

"Mr. Hale, those birds must go. They are interfering with the Lord's worship."

"Quite to the contrary, sir," objected grandfather, "they are doing the Lord's work in preventing me, and I hope others, from listening to your false and obnoxious doctrines."

"Then I'll have the law on you for this," blustered the reverend.

"I know of no law, sir," countered my grandfather, "which forbids a goose gabbling or a cock crowing or for that matter," and here he pointed his finger at the enraged divine, "a jack-ass from braying."

Beside himself now with anger and frustration, the minister turned to go with a parting vitriolic shot.

"May I say, Mr. Hale, I consider it most unseemly and a shameful example for these children (by that time my father's two older half-brothers had appeared) that an old man of 75 years who has already buried two wives should marry a young woman of 32 and" this last he spat out contemptuously," have a baby!'"

This was too much for grandfather.

"Sir," he shouted, "if it weren't for your cloth, I'd kick you off my property. Now, get out!"

Whether he couldn't compete further with the geese, but probably for other reasons since grandfather was not without influence, the minister did not remain long in Glastonbury after this battle.

Grandfather lost his last argument — that with an oak log which he was trying to split — in his 91st year, leaving my father his only child, a boy of 15. While I never knew my grandfather, through his portrait I have grown to feel a kind of continuous presence and even solicitude — a post mortal understanding, if you will. So when I stand before it occasionally and whisper, "Pekin geese" it seems as if the stern countenance moved slightly in a flicker of a smile.

CHAPTER 19

The Yankee Peddler

The early settlers of Connecticut had to be self sufficient in providing for their needs. The family was essentially a self contained entity in itself. All the family food, except such few luxuries as sugar, tea and coffee, when they could be secured, was raised, the clothing was woven or knit by the wife and daughters, wood to keep warm and for cooking. was cut and stored by the men. The man of the family had to be an ingenious jack-of-all-trades with the ability to contrive repairs and replacements, and invent new implements and devices to accomplish his purposes and keep his simple economy in operation.

Some settlers, shoemakers, blacksmiths, masons, carpenters and the like, brought their trades from England and taught them to sons and apprentices, but the many products developed under the harsh necessities of New England life grew largely out of family activities, and the unusual quality or effectiveness of some family product like an animal trap, a leather strop or harness, an apple parer, a clock, or clothes pin.

Waste has above all things been abhorrent to the Yankee. In the economy of New England, whether it be crops out of her rocky soil, warmth out of her oaks, or milk and meat out of her animals, all such things are the result of hard work. "Wanton waste brings woeful want" was a warning embroidered on many a sampler. The New Englander hates to waste his time, and is always looking for an easier way to do things. He will spend a long time considering a problem in an attempt to solve it at the least expenditure of effort. To some this appears to verge on laziness, but actually it is the root reason why Connecticut men have for generations and still take out more patents each year than any other similar section of the country.

The industries that began in the farmhouse, in the mill by the pond, in a country barn or kitchen, or metal working shop had an innate vitality and a hungry market which were brought together by the peddler. At first, the tendency was for the peddler to carry only the one item, made by his family or by a small group. Thus Amos Stanley of New Britain made hats, took them west and bartered them for beaver skins and other pelts, and returned to make more hats. Another planted some broom corn, made and sold to neighbors a few brooms, and each year increased his acreage and the area of his market.

The works for grandfather clocks were imported, and the purchaser had to build the case himself. So Eli Terry started making wooden parts and the complete shelf clock. By 1837, he had started stamping the parts out of brass, assisted by a young apprentice, Seth Thomas from West Haven. Soon peddlers were carrying these to every town and village. Brass buttons were made in Waterbury in 1750, and they are made there today. The early peddlers of silverware from Wallingford and Meriden apparently sold nothing else. As roads improved and it was possible to push a hand cart or to use horse and cart, peddlers became independent of the individual manufacturer and took on as varied a line of goods as can be found in a small department store.

Jewelry from Attleboro, silks from Manchester,

clocks from Bristol, locks from New Britain, silver from Wallingford, bells from East Hampton, the list is almost endless. At the end of the era, articles peddled included drugs, patent medicines, indigo for dyeing from the Carolinas, Bennington crockery, baskets, brooms, dress goods, laces and notions, hardware, tin ware, Paisley shawls — you name it, he had it somewhere in his trunk or cart.

As bone buttons supplanted the metal buttons of colonial times, E. C. Maltby of Northford made buttons out of bone, ivory, horn and wood, and maintained four peddlers on the road. As already recounted in this column, other Wallingford manufacturers, especially of silver plate, distributed their wares throughout the settled areas of the country through peddlers. As one commentator expresses it, "Meriden became — only because it served as a peddlers' headquarters." And into what distant places went Samuel Colt's revolver — originated out of his brain and modeled in wood on shipboard when he was twenty years old?

David Bushnell of Westbrook couldn't peddle his product, the first submarine about 1777, but they are still turned out in Connecticut a short distance from their birthplace. Would you know of the glories of Connecticut's inventive genius and other virtues, read Odell Shepard's "Connecticut: Past and Present" which should be required reading for every high school student to give him a basic pride in his state to last a lifetime.

It is probable that I am among the few people in town — possibly the only one — who remembers seeing an authentic tin peddler's cart operating on the streets of Wallingford. The time was about 1895, and I was old enough to mark it as an unusual sight. The cart was in front of my home on So. Main St., now the site of the Post Office building, painted, as was customary, a bright red, and almost completely covered with an array of pails, tubs, pans and similar articles . Actually by 1895 the era of the tin peddler had passed and this one was perhaps carrying on his work in the pleasant summertime more for his own love of the open road than for profit, because by that time the economic reasons for that kind of merchandising had elapsed.

On the other hand most peddlers evolved regular routes and stopping places, established social relations with customers and in the villages often joined in the dances and parties, sometimes providing the music, and obviously were generally welcomed as honest men. The dishonest salesman rarely returns to the scene of the crime. Let it be said the Yankee peddler traded hard but with exceptions doubtless magnified, was generally as fair as the times and circumstances permitted.

For it was a hard life, away from home, buffeted by all kinds of weather, and meeting and overcoming daily almost insuperable obstacles. He had to be his own doctor, and many times for other people, he usually did his own cooking, and had to have mechanical skill when his wheel broke or in repairing for resale articles taken in trade. In short he had to be resourceful in emergencies, pleasant in manner, loquacious with gossip-starved women, knowledgeable in politics and farm matters with the men, merry with the children and attractive to the girls. A big order for any young fellow.

But to the young men on the Connecticut farms with the large families of the period crowding the house the opportunity to escape and see the world by peddling some neighbor's wares was too good to be overlooked For nearly 100 years, a large number of such young men started out from home each year, at first with baskets, packs or trunks, later with hand carts and ultimately with horse and wagon to earn their living and incidentally to travel to the then far places of their small world.

Young Bronson Alcott, later to be father of the Alcott sisters of "Little Women" fame and one of New England's brightest intellects, left his birthplace in nearby Wolcott in the fall of 1823 and with 15 other men and a tinsmith sailed from New Haven to Norfolk, Va. From that point as headquarters they spread out and travelled over the Southern states during the winter. Indeed it was a common saying that Connecticut peddlers were "as thick as toads after a rain." Especially after the Revolution youth became restless and we read "Whereas formerly apprentices and young folk kept the Sabbath, now they go out more on the Sabbath than any other day. They say it is better than going to church to sit two hours and hear about Hell." Apparently youth found the parental yoke just as galling in 1790 as in 1970 and seized upon a chance for freedom and the open road.

The spirit of adventure was everywhere. One young peddler encountered John Jacob Astor out searching for furs and went along with him to Canada. Some joined in the gold rush to California in 1849. Marshall Field grew tired of peddling and settled down in Chicago. Later Benjamin Altman and Adam Gimbel, peddlers both, did the same in New York. Meyer Guggenheim who had carried his goods on his back through the mining districts of Pennsylvania around 1847, turned to mining himself and amassed a fabulous fortune in copper. Another Connecticut Yankee, Benedict Arnold, peddled woolen goods for his father-in-law up the Hudson and into Canada, thus doubtless familiarizing himself with West Point and Quebec, destined to become his shame and his glory respectively. Collis P. Huntington, as a young fellow from Connecticut, peddled through the South and West, joined the gold rush, set up store in Sacramento, and made millions in linking California to the East by railroad. And finally, B. T. Babbit sold razor strops, very likely made in Wallingford.

The epoch of the Yankee peddler reached its zenith in the period following the Revolution until 1830. At that time the oppressive marriage laws in Bavaria set in motion an emigration of German Jews to America. Used to the hardship, the unremitting labor and the privations of the ghetto and with bargaining instinct, sharpened to a razor's edge by generations of bartering, they found the peddler's life in America a comparatively easy one. More of their compatriots followed after the German revolution of 1848. The Yankee peddler as such was doomed in any event by the coming of railroads, turnpikes, the steamboat, and the growth of cities and towns with ample merchandising facilities. The economic conditions which had created the Yankee peddler had ceased to exist. He was to be succeeded by the traveling salesman who was to use the railroad to carry both himself and his sample case and trunk. Henceforth the Yankee for the most part stayed at home to manufacture his wares, or retired from peddling to a general store in some community where he had found a girl to share his life and fortunes.

Aside from the picturesque and romantic aspects of the era of the Yankee peddler, it had great historical significance. He was one of the main influences in opening up the West to settlement for the peddler was not far behind the trapper and explorer. Indeed an instance is recorded when some explorers happened upon a group of peddlers with three wagons loaded with all kinds of trumpery, cheap beads and jewelry and knick-knacks which they were trading with the Indians for furs. Peddlers at times, probably justly, were charged with supplying the Indians with guns and liquor, the latter being a great help in the bargaining.

In any event, peddlers served as scouts in virgin territory, bringing back to New England information about the fertile plains. No wonder the farmer trying to scratch a living out of his rocky upland pastures and fields decided to pack up and go West. The back roads of Connecticut and New England bear witness in the stone walls winding over the rocky hills to the early farms abandoned for the lush fields of Ohio. In the brief period between the Revolution and 1800 some 500,000 people moved from the Eastern seaboard to western New York, Ohio, Virginia and Kentucky, thus spreading

New England seed and culture through the Middle West.

Because Wallingford used the Yankee peddler so effectively to promote its products, some of which have been the backbone of the town's growth and prosperity, because Wallingford over the years has been the home of hundreds who have spent much of their lives in travel as representatives for our industries, because I myself spent ten years on the road peddling securities, and for nearly 50 years directed the activities of dozens of salesmen, and most of all perhaps because as a Yankee I take pride in the historical importance of their work, their pertinacity and other virtues, the Yankee peddler has had a peculiar fascination for me.

Thus I have never forgotten that red cart on Main St., nor another but related field of salesmanship, the "Medicine Man," who used to tie up his horse and wagon in front of the present Dime Savings Bank and under a flaring torch bring forward a figure clad in full Indian attire and introduce him as the discoverer of that remedy for all ills — at only fifty cents a bottle — the "Kick-a-poo Indian" tonic. I never bought any so I am in the dark as to the nature of the concoction, but I believe it was made in the old brick building in Clintonville and consisted of 60% alcohol with the rest nearby Muddy River water.

When all is said and done, even the wooden nutmeg was just another manifestation of the Yankees' ingenuity and resourcefulness, when he had to "make do," and of his dry sense of humor, for what could be dryer than grated wooden nutmeg?

CHAPTER 20

The Stepping Stone

"How I hate that woman," thought Rosie Callahan as Mrs. Slate walked toward the door of the shop, her bustle moving rhythmically from side to side and imparting a swishing sound with each step as her petticoats swept the floor.

Rose Callahan's dislike had deeper roots than the natural jealousy of those with less for those with more of almost everything. Back in the early 1850's Patrick O'Brien had come to Wallingford from Ireland with his wife and 11-year-old Rosie. Within five years he had been killed by a cave-in on a construction job. His wife supported herself and Rosie by taking in washing, but a typhoid epidemic brought her death, and Rosie, an orphan at 18, married young Timmie Callahan.

It seemed that now her troubles were over, but in 1863 the Civil War was at its worst with the draft taking men right and left. A Yankee family up town offered Timmie a $300 bounty to take the place of their son, and off he went to war. He fell at Chancellorsville.

So Rosie, left a widow at 20, went to work at Wallace's packing tin spoons for the army. The 12-hour day was long and tiring, but Rosie was young and strong, the place neighborly, and once in a while Mr. Robert and his two little boys, Henry and Frank, would stop by her bench for a chat.

It was at this dull period in her life that she met young Tom Slate, a clerk in an uptown store. There

were quiet times when they walked by Community
Lake, and great occasions when he hired a horse and
buggy and took her down to the Three Elm House in
Stony Creek for a shore dinner. Indeed a friend of
Tom's who was haying in a field they passed quizzed
Tom about his girl being sick and having to be held in
the buggy. So Rose might have entertained hopes that
her widowhood would end except that it was, of course,
unthinkable for a good Catholic girl to marry a blue
nosed Yankee Protestant.

So when Rosie heard that Tom was engaged to
marry Georgianna Whittelsey, she wasn't too surprised
although her heart sank and privately she wept a few
tears. The Whittelseys had money, and not long after
Tom bought the ownership of the store.

Several years later at a band concert on Saturday
night Tom happened to meet Rosie and after chatting a
while, by no means oblivious to her blue eyes, curly
black hair, creamy complexion and buxom figure, he
said:

"Rosie, I need a clerk in the store. Helen Hall is
leaving to get married. How would you like the job? I
can pay you $15 a week."

That was $3.00 more than she was receiving in the
factory, clerking was much more interesting than
packing spoons, and besides it was lady's work. So she
accepted.

Working with Tom was pleasant, she liked to meet
and talk with people that came in to shop, and most of
all she liked the feeling of the bolts of silk and wool as
she measured them out yard by yard on the brass
buttons set in the counter for the ladies to have made
up by their dress makers. Furthermore, as the years
passed, she had to admit to herself she liked more and
more being with Tom.

Her one source of unhappiness was Mrs. Slate who
took it upon herself to visit the store every day, and
invariably find some reason to reprove Rosie, perhaps
for leaving a bolt of cloth partly unrolled on the counter

after a just departed customer, perhaps because some thread was in the wrong drawer, or even because her unruly curly black hair was untidy. The truth was Mrs. Slate knew of Tom's previous attentions to Rosie and being herself small and scrawny was jealous and would gladly have had her discharged. Indeed the matter had become one for constant bickering between husband and wife and as time went on this friction produced a domestic heat that threatened to burst into flame at any moment.

But as it happened one winter diptheria ran rampant through the town and Mrs. Slate died. Tom maintained the proper year of mourning and then began to ask Rosie to go out with him again, to the minstrels in New Haven, to the fairs, and to small parties with his friends. So she had had ample time to think and was not surprised when he asked her to marry him but her long frustration had left a bitter taste. Yes, she said, she had always loved him, but her pride had been dragged in the mud so long that she needed to have it restored to make a proper wife for him so she set two conditions: she would not live in the house where Mrs. Slate had lived so Tom must build her a new one, something elegant like the Beach house, but not so large. He gladly agreed.

"There's one thing more, Tom," she said firmly. "That woman has bedeviled me all my life, and so far as I can tell she has made it hell for you. You never really loved her, and I hated her, and she deserved it. Tom, I want that tombstone you had set up in the cemetery brought and placed along the driveway to the new house, so when I go out to drive in my carriage, I can step on it as I get in and out. When the house is finished and the stone in place I will marry you.

— — — — — — — — —

If you chance to stroll down So. Main St. some afternoon, you will see on the west side a large square house with a beautiful wrought iron fence in the lyre pattern set in cut stone running along in front. The gates, unfrotunately, are gone, but the whole effect is one of shabby gentility, a kind of decayed grandeur.

If then you will enter the yard and go around to the rear you will see a large block of sandstone and on one side an undecipherable inscription.

Mrs. Schember, who lived across the street, a woman of unimpeachable veracity, used to watch the second Mrs. Slate mount the stone and enter her carriage and she used to tell callers in a hushed and horrified voice.

"When she got out, she always turned and spit on it."

CHAPTER 21

The Civil War

When I was a boy in the 1890's the memories of the Civil War were still fresh in the minds of everyone. That family which had not suffered in one way or another was rare, and my mother's older brother, Delavan, had died at 23 of exposure in an army camp. The men who at ages from 18 to 25 had fought the war were now in prime of life and prominent in the business and civic life of the community.

We boys were consequently always fighting the war over again in our play, and the background of our reading consisted largely of adventure stories based on the war like Harry Castleman's series — Frank on the River, Frank Before Vicksburg, etc. — Cudjo's Cave, Jed and many similar tales. My special pet was Campfire and Battleground, a history of the war profusely illustrated with the Brady photographs.

The Grand Army of the Republic, or G.A.R. as it was always called, like the present American Legion and Veterans of Foreign Wars, took an active part in political affairs — all Republican infighting — and especially in the celebration of Memorial Day and other national holidays. Prior to Memorial Day, the veterans individually or in small groups visited the schools and gave vivid accounts of life in the army.

Eighteen Wallingford men responded to Lincoln's first call for volunteers and fought at Bull Run. Apparently some continued to serve during the war, but early enlistments were for short duration, the enthusiasm soon cooled, and as the war settled down to the usual components of hardship, suffering and defeat, men became subject to draft. It is typical of the changes brought about in a century that it was then possible for a draftee to hire a substitute to go to war for him. The going rate for such substitutes was $300.

Over the five year duration of the Civil War several hundred men from Wallingford served at one time or another after the original company K left for action. About 180 veterans are recorded as buried here, and of course, many were buried where they fell in military cemeteries and some in other towns.

Certainly Wallingford along with the whole country North and South suffered grievously. The list of battles on the Soldiers Monument shows that Wallingford men fought in most of the bloodiest conflicts of the war — Antietam, Chancellorsville and Gettysburg among them.

The most prominent figure from Wallingford was Colonel Arthur H. Dutton whose brilliant military record was recognized in the naming after him of the local G.A.R. Post and Dutton Park. The Soldiers Monument and the park were dedicated in 1902, the former being unveiled by Mrs. Margaret Tibbits Taber, while I observed the ceremony from a neighboring tree.

Soon after the Civil War broke out, Moses Yale Beach presented to the town a Liberty Pole 150 feet tall which was erected in the center of the junction of Main and Center streets. In the accompanying photograph the pole is shown at the extreme left. The large building stood on the southeast corner and during my boyhood was always referred to as "the old corner house."

Originally built as an inn, it was situated on So. Orchard St. below Parsons St. At that time Parsons St., winding up the hill from the Old Colony Rd., was the main entrance to the town from the south. Sometime prior to 1861, when the photograph was taken, the building was hauled by teams of oxen all the way to its

final site where it remained until the first post office building was erected there in 1913. I remember the late Charles H. Tibbits remarking on the extravagance of the United States in spending $250,000 for that structure. What a contrast to the $4,000,000 spent for the present ugly, graceless eyesore. O tempora, O mores!

Memorial Day in the 1890's as I remember it was always sunny and sometimes very warm. I recall one year when my friends in the "Boys Brigade" of the Congregational Church (there were no Boy Scouts then), tightly encased in heavily padded dress uniforms collapsed after marching and standing in the sun for several hours.

A pleasantly numerous crowd milled around the center while the parade was forming, sprinkled with men in blue uniforms and slouch hats carrying the G.A.R. emblem and women with great baskets of lilacs and other flowers for decorating the graves. The lilacs I remember particularly because so infrequently in recent years have lilacs been in bloom on Memorial Day. Despite weather records which apparently show little change I am convinced spring was later a century ago, and certainly we saw no cardinals in winter and rarely if ever in summer. It may well be that pollution of the atmosphere is gradually converting us to a greenhouse era!

Unless my memory tricks me, Botsford's saloon was open on Memorial Day and did a land office business as the boys in blue lined up to treat each other and prepare for the hot trek down and up Center St. hill and then up to In Memoriam Cemetery and back again, not to mention the long and perhaps dry oration of the day.

The parade usually consisted of the Wallingford band leading, followed by the company of G.A.R. veterans, and then a motley crowd of women and children with the Yalesville Drum Corps conspicuous in the midst. Captain Dan Barber in his uniform and Baron Lothar von Grave in his Knights Templar regalia, mounted on spirited saddle horses, added color to the occasion.

The Civil War was not fought for personal power or economic advantage but with the issue clearly defined and the ultimate result the end which had been sought in the beginning. Memorial Day today is soured by acrimony over the past political and military bumbling which have cost the lives of 40,000 more young men to be mourned. On the contrary Memorial Day in the 1890's was filled with the nostalgia of an earlier and simpler era and sad sweetness like the subtle scent of lilacs of the memory of sons or lovers lost in a noble cause.

CHAPTER 22

The Wallingford Community

It is a curious paradox that Vermont, reputedly the home of moral virtue and strict religious views, should have given birth to the two men who formulated and built into national prominence social and religious movements utterly alien and obnoxious to their upbringing and their times. With Brigham Young and the Mormons Wallingford had no direct associations, but John Humphrey Noyes was for years a familiar and controversial figure on the local scene.

Noyes was pure New England, and Simon-pure Vermont in background and breeding. He was the scion of an odd, clannish, ingrown, repressed and in fact downright peculiar family, the members so bashful, shy and introspective that they usually married their own cousins. John Noyes may well be considered to have been the flower of this century plant of inhibitions or the volcano which finally erupted from the pent up passions beneath the stark and forbidding Vermont exterior.

He was born in the small village of Atkinson, Vt. in 1811. His father was a dour man, a successful merchant and a representative in Congress who did not marry until 36 years old; his mother was a woman of high intelligence, great industry and with deep religious roots and convictions on the most orthodox lines. Young Noyes followed his father to Dartmouth and was graduated with Phi Beta Kappa standing. Strongly motivated by his mother's training, he entered the seminary at Andover to train for the ministry, but becoming quickly disillusioned by the regimen and the intellectual poverty of his fellow students, he transferred to Yale where he was graduated in Divinity in 1833 and licensed to preach. For several years he remained in New Haven, developing his doctrine of "Perfectionism," forming a free church, and setting up a press to spread his religious theories. It was during this period that he became familiar with Wallingford.

"Perfectionism" in essence was the doctrine that man could by his own efforts attain a sinless existence. Theologically, this was anathema to the orthodox doctrines of the time which were based on original sin and saving by grace. Noyes immediately became not only persona non grata to his associates in the ministry, but the object of contumely and active hostility.

In New Haven, Noyes met Miss Abigail Merwin, a young woman of excellent family and eight years his senior. His efforts to engage her interest in him and his theories were thwarted by her family, and she eventually married. Even so, some years later Noyes followed her out to Ithaca, N.Y. where he spent several years, but made no progress in his suit. Certainly this long and frustrating wooing had a tremendous psychological impact from which may well have developed Noyes' theories on "Complex Marriage" which basically denied exclusive marital privileges.

Noyes may be considered the epitome of a man of his time. The decade from 1830 to 1840 was one of extreme religious and philosophical ferment. Robert Owens of England had expounded his theories of a Utopian Commonwealth. It was the era of sects like the Millerites who preached the approaching end of the world, gave away all their property and on a certain night went up on a hilltop to await the final judgment. This decade marked the birth of Universalism and Transcendentalism. The imported cult of Sweden Borgianism became a popular topic of discussion. The

Shakers had set up their villages where all shared the common lot in a setting of sexual abstinence. Emerson, Hawthorne and the Concord group were busily engaged with the social experiment of Brook Farm, and to top it all off the Abolitionists were in full cry to wipe out slavery.

That Noyes, seething with resentment against the hypocricies and repressions of the orthodox religious authorities and rejected in love, should have been swirled along and tossed high in this flood of social and religious heresies, this breaking up of frozen streams engaging the deepest human emotions, is not strange. Coupling a zealous intensity of Messianic fire with an almost hypnotic power over men often and women almost invariably he began to set his theories in motion throughout New England and New York.

In pursuing his doctrine of "Perfectionism" Noyes came face to face with that old demon, sex. He overcame this by the simple expedient of wiping away any stigma of sin and substituting the idea that since love was the motivating influence, no sin was incurred. Indeed on the contrary sexual intercourse should be encouraged. The methods employed by Noyes and his associates to enjoy all the benefit of amativeness without suffering from a population explosion I leave to the pornographically curious. If, however, you think that because Noyes was familiar with the Bible, he followed the example of Onan, you are mistaken.

By 1851, the year the Wallingford Community was started, Noyes, then 40 years old, was at the height of his efforts to convert the world by preaching and press to the practice of "Perfectionism." In this he had as might be expected encountered insuperable obstacles and suffered physically and mentally from failure and disappointment. He had, however, succeeded in establishing a relatively firm base at Oneida, N.Y. though it was subject to sporadic harassment from the authorities.

In the year 1851, a man named Henry Allen had a

small farm on the site of the present Masonic Home. Becoming convinced from reading the Noyes' tracts that the doctrines promulgated were sound and applicable to himself, his wife and four children, he invited members of the Noyes Community at Oneida, N.Y. to join with himself and other local converts in the formation of a branch Community upon his land. It was a pleasant and sightly spot. Through the meadows below wound the Quinnipiac River, and beyond the sand plains studded with oaks rose a ridge along which stretched the village of Wallingford. The tracks of the recently built New Haven Railroad made a straight line of silver steel across the plain, and an occasional house on the Old Colony Road was visible through the trees.

The invitation to come to Wallingford was accepted, and some members from Oneida with the Wallingford contingent made up a group of modestly well-to-do and hard-working people. There are those still living in Wallingford whose relatives of the earlier generation were among the members. From the original small farm and simple farm house the holdings of the Community increased over the next 25 years to some 240 acres.

Here the Community maintained itself by farming, and raising and peddling vegetables and fruit in the vicinity. Later they branched into such staples as pins and needles, lace edging and various products handmade by the individual members. (I must digress at this point to mention that on some of our pillow slips is such lace edging or tatting as it was called by my grandmother some seventy years ago, and it is still fresh and strong.)

The river flowing by the front door naturally intrigued such practical people as a source of power. A dam was built at the north end of the present lake, and a race-way or mill-race dug along the east bank of the river to supply power to a small mill. Farther downstream, Robert Wallace was already busily engaged in making spoons and needed more power. Accordingly, he made an arrangement with the Community to build a new dam at the present site, and thus Community or Lake Windemere as it was then called was formed.

The raising of the lake level transformed a point of higher land on the west side just opposite the present Exchange baseball field into an island of considerable size. This was promptly named "Paradise Island," connected to the shore by a board walk on raised piers, and became a favorite place for picnics and a base for water sports. The last raising of the dam and the water level wiped out this pleasant resort of the gay 90's.

Life did not run smoothly for the Wallingford Community though it never suffered the slings and arrows directed against Oneida. It was more a matter of mere existence in the years after its founding and during the Civil War. It did perform the function of serving as a nearby home and retreat for the young men from other Communities during their years at Yale, an institution apparently favored by Noyes by reason of his previous connections.

Then disaster struck the Community in the form of a persistent epidemic of malarial fever. Many members were sickened, some died, and others went back to Oneida to escape. Malaria laid a miasma of fear over Wallingford for many years. I remember as a small boy my mother kept my bedroom window closed at night "to keep out the malaria." As its name indicates, this disease was then popularly supposed to emanate from exhalations of swampy areas. Science now knows, of course, that like yellow fever malaria is transmitted by the bite of an infected mosquito. So my mother was right in that she excluded the mosquitoes with the air!

The financial depression of the 70's and the malaria sounded the death knell for the Community. The printing house which used the water power in which the Community had sunk almost $100,000 was closed and the water power idle. There was one final effort. Charles Cragin, son of an original Community couple, educated at Yale as a mechanical engineer, would not accept defeat. As he sat disconsolately on the dam one morning in 1877 watching the water pour over in wasted energy he heard the crashing sounds of the hammers from the Wallace factory below punching out spoons. The thought came that here in a closed factory and wasted power were the means for doing the same thing: all he needed was some equipment. John Noyes found the means to provide it, and soon the Community was supplying large quantities of spoons to the Meriden Britannia Company.

Encouraged by this success, Noyes tore down the original farm house and erected a more commodious building on the same site, still remembered by local residents. But this spurt was short-lived. Noyes went back to Oneida to deal with the difficulties there, and within a few months Cragin was dead of the dread malaria. His work lived after him and became the nucleus of the present prosperous Oneida Community Silver Co. This was the final blow to the Wallingford Community. The property was sold, eventually to come into the possession of the Masonic Order, and serve as a basis for the great institution of today.

For the next 15 years, Noyes was on the defensive against attacks by public opinion and the law that regarded his theory and practice of complex marriage as completely immoral, and finally sought refuge in Canada where he died on April 13, 1886. The ultimate blow in the dissolution of the Community as such came, however, from within in the form of a youthful revolution against John Noyes' final experiment in human beings – the practice of stirpiculture.

This idea was the culmination of John Noyes' theories in human relationships and their results. In essence it provided for the selection of the best males in the Community and their mating with the best females with the expectation of producing a superior race in mental and physical characteristics. But since Noyes and his older associates naturally considered themselves the compendium and epitome of male excellence and were mated with the youngest and prettiest of the feminine members while the young men had to find such consolation as they could in the older females beyond child bearing, youth rebelled at such a raw deal. Noyes was exiled, the communistic theories were abandoned, and a corporation formed to take over the thriving animal trap and silver industries.

John Humphrey Noyes was an iconoclast in religion and morals, and suffered the fate of all who smash the idols of the orthodox. He sought to release physical love from its procreative palliative, and to combine this freedom with a sharing of the fruits of labor among the whole group. Noyes as an individual who could deny the claims of the strongest human emotions could not understand why such doctrines should meet the inflexible opposition not only of church and state but of the general public. Complex marriage had a basis of ethical principles which makes the present divorce rate take on a shameful aspect. Read "Brave New World" and you will find Aldous Huxley picturing stirpiculture in full flower.

Wallingford cannot claim the honor or the infamy of John Noyes' birth or even of his citizenship, but for a period of nearly half a century he was a frequent visitor, and his was a household albeit a whispered name. He had the genius of all great men — we now call it charisma — to inspire the allegiance of men and women in a cause that could only be subject to ridicule and harassment.

Had it not been for the epidemic of malaria, the business enterprises he started a century ago could be thriving here today and Noyes' name be inscribed with those of Wallace and Simpson as founders of Wallingford industry. As it is, only the name of the lovely lake on which Noyes used to gaze as he rocked on the verandah of the Community House remains to mark his struggles and defeat.

CHAPTER 23

Set-back

"It's always a good idea," said Cousin Walter, "to look a job over carefully before you start working."

We were sitting on his front porch after lunch and the object of his remark was the meadow across the road where the newcut hay was drying in the July sun.

"Now just take that apple tree over there," he pointed to a dilapidated up-rooted growth behind the barn where a stump and some broken branches emerged from a tangle of briars. "That tree must have blown down ten years ago, and I've been thinking ever since about how best to tackle cutting it up. It begins to look as if the problem would settle itself, and the whole thing just gradually disappear."

He was silent for awhile, then said, "As you grow older, Clarence, you'll appreciate how many problems just disappear if you let them alone." He glanced at me as if trying to figure out from my expression just how much of this Yankee drollery I was swallowing.

"Now that job across the road is different," he continued. "If we let that hay lie there while I decide the best way to get it in, we're likely to run into a spell of wet weather and spoil it. So I guess we'll just have to tackle it the old fashioned way without any improvement. Besides, the keeper will be out any minute and shoo us off the porch."

"What's a keeper, Cousin Walter?" I inquired.

"Well, there's bee-keepers, inn-keepers, house-keepers, store-keepers, and jail-keepers, to name a few, but the one I referred to you might call a husband-keeper."

As Cousin Walter continued his contemplation of the meadow, a smile crinkled the corner of his mouth and finally he remarked: "I've meant for sometime to put a marker over there — the Willie Andrews Athletic Field — but I haven't got round to it."

"Why do you call it that?" I asked .

"It's quite a long story, Clarence, but I'll try to shorten it up." He hesitated and I thought he was overcome by emotion, but I discovered he was shaking with inward laughter.

"Perhaps you don't know that us farmers after a hard day like to get together for a game of set-back. One night in November, some years back, my brother, Del, Willie Andrews, 'Epe' Peck and I were having a game right here in the house."

"Wait a minute," I interrupted, "I never heard that name 'Epe' before."

"Well, it wasn't his name, really. It's funny how cruel parents can be to children, but his named him Epaphroditus. I guess they wanted to balance the short name with a long one, so he could learn to walk earlier. Now take your name, that's a real pretty one." He looked at me with a rather odd glance like a pitcher putting a strike over an inside corner.

"Well, as I was saying," he went on, "set-back is what you would call a hilarious game, and to maintain a proper level there's nothing so helpful as cider that's been setting awhile. This particular game was a tough one, and as the evening went on I had occasion to bring up several pitchers full from the barrel in the cellar. I remember once when Willie won a hand, he banged his fist down on the table and the cider went right up out of the glass and hit the ceiling. The spot's there now."

The screen door behind us opened and Cousin Harriet stuck her head out.

"You boys better get going or you won't get that hay in tonight." She projected the words like bullets out of a machine gun and shut the door with a bang.

"We're going right along," answered Cousin Walter, "I was just telling Clarence about Willie Andrews." He winked at me and whispered, "She'll be out again pretty soon, so I'll have to hurry."

His body started shaking again as if laughter was boiling inside like water in a tea kettle.

"That game went on till near midnight and Willie got so

sleepy he slipped right down under the table, so we laid him
out on the couch. When the boys got ready to leave we shook
him up and got him on his feet, but he was pretty groggy,"
he corrected himself with a glance at me — "sleepy, I
mean."

"I helped the boys on with their coats and Del and Epe
went along and left me to take care of Willie. By that time
there was one of those early November snow squalls and it
was coming down hard. So I got Willie down off the porch
here and started him out straight for the barn where his
horse was hitched. I went in the house and started putting
things to rights, no small job, and was on my way upstairs
when there was a rap at the door. I went down and opened
up and there was Willie."

Cousin Walter paused as if to sum up in his mind the
horror of the scene.

"Willie," he continued, "was smeared from head to foot
with a mixture of snow, mud and dead grass. His hat was
gone and his eyes were kind of scared looking."

Walt," he said, and his voice was all choked up, "I can't
find my rig."

"Why, Willie," I reassured him, "if it ain't been stolen,
it's right where you left it at the barn. Come on, we'll go
see."

"So I took his arm, walked him out to the barn, and
there was his horse and buggy all right. So I helped him in,
unhitched the horse and led her down to the road and aimed
her for home. I knew she'd take Willie right into his yard
but, of course, she couldn't wake him up and undress him so
I guess he spent the night in the carriage."

"Next morning was clear and bright, and I'd forgot to
get the mail the day before so I went down to the road early.
As I looked down on the meadow I saw where the sun had
already melted some spots that zig-zagged all over that
white field. It all come to me what happened. Willie had slid
straight down the bank beyond the road and then wandered
round in the snow just missing falling into the brook."

Just then the screen door opened again and Cousin
Harriet came out with a broom in her hand. "Now scat, you
two. You've been sitting here half an hour." "All right,
we're going," said Cousin Walter, getting to his feet.

As we crossed the road he continued, "Willie always

said it was just a nightmare he had where he was cast into an Arctic sea, swam until he saw a lighthouse, then got in a boat and rowed ashore. When I showed him his hat I picked up under the bank he couldn't deny it 'cause it had two pitchfork holes through it where he lost it in the hay one summer and didn't find it till the next year."

"Cousin Walter," I said, "I don't believe I'd put up any marker after all. I don't think Mr. Andrews would like to be reminded he was drunk."

He looked at me with a mixture of surprise and amusement. "I guess I misjudged you, Clarence," he finally commented. "We'll forget all about it."

CHAPTER 24

Giants in the Land

When Captain William Mix of Prospect hired two bright and already work-hardened farm boys as apprentices in his small metal working shop he could have had no possible thought, let alone expectation, that he was presiding at the birth of two great silver dynasties. Over a hundred years later the grandsons of these boys after spending their lives in the industry were to live and die as close friends and next door neighbors.

Late in the 18th century, one James Wallace came from Scotland to Blandford, Mass. He was a silk weaver, and brought with him looms on which he manufactured silk stockings. His son, James, moved to Prospect, Conn., where he had a farm. It was his son, Robert, who is the hero of our story.

From the time he was nine years old Robert worked on his father's and neighboring farms, snatching such fragmentary schooling as he could. At 16 he was apprenticed to Captain Mix, and after two years of picking up the fundamentals of making various metal products he went into business for himself in an old grist mill in Cheshire. Soon after he had started, a Mr. Sherman of New Haven showed him a spoon made of a strange metal, called German silver from the country of its origin.

The industrial genius, ingenuity, alertness, and

driving force of Robert Wallace were immediately apparent. Bear in mind that he was only 19 years old. Obtaining from Mr. Sherman the name of the German chemist in New York with whom Mr. Sherman had been in contact, Wallace went to New York and succeeded in buying a bar of the metal. Returning home, he rolled the bar and made some four dozen spoons. Samples of these he showed to Mr. Hall of Hall, Elton & Co. and together they started making the first German or, as it was later termed, nickel silver.

The next step was to secure the formula for making the metal in which Wallace was successful, buying nickel in New York, and arranging for further imports from Germany. It was during this period that Robert Wallace bought the mill and water power at Quinnie, close to the Southern town line on the Quinnipiac. This was an industrial site for some 200 years, starting with a grist mill in the earliest years of the town. Later wood screws, razor strops and other articles were manufactured there, and after Wallace outgrew the facilities paper and bolts were made until finally it was purchased by the town in 1905 for its electric light plant.

In 1854, the west lured Robert Wallace away, but only briefly and he returned to enter partnership with Samuel Simpson. This lasted 10 years when a corporation was formed owned one-third by Wallace, one-third by Simpson, and one-third by the Meriden Britannia Co. At that time – 1865 – the first of the buildings on the present site was built. Five years later Wallace bought Samuel Simpson's one-third interest and with control firmly in his own hands, the name became R. Wallace and Sons. In 1875 the manufacture of sterling silver, in which Wallace was to become pre-eminent, began.

Until his death in 1892 Robert Wallace continued to expand the business with the increasing assistance of his sons, Henry and Frank, his sons-in-law, Colonel W. J. Leavenworth and Dennis Morris and eventually the third generation.

For well over a century now the industry established and built up by Robert Wallace has given employment to a large segment of the town's people, and has made the name of Wallingford known throughout the country. The life of this man, remarkable for his energy, the vigor and intellectual capacity of his mind, and his executive ability, all in a frame of moral integrity, was in the best American tradition of his era.

The career of David S. Stevens closely paralleled that of Robert Wallace. After completing his apprenticeship with Captain Mix in Prospect he moved on to various jobs around the State, but returned to Wallingford and formed a partnership with Wallace at his Quinnie plant. However, in 1869 he moved to Northford where he set up his own plant and continued until 1880.

In the meantime back in 1837, Hall, Elton and Company was busily turning out tin spoons. To Deacon Almer Hall, young Robert Wallace showed a sample of his German silver spoon. Recognizing at once the superior quality of the metal, Mr. Hall arranged with Wallace to make the spoons in quantity.

As the business increased, Hall, Elton bought the factory at the foot of Community Lake, left empty by the departure of the Wallingford Community. Some time later, Hall, Elton moved to the square building across from the railroad station now occupied by the Bartek Co. In my many years of use of the railroad station I never failed to look with sentimental interest at this building since my father started work there when he came to Wallingford in 1879 as a young man of 22.

This move by Hall, Elton opened the door for Elizur Seneca Stevens, son of David Stevens, to buy the former Hall, Elton plant where he continued his father's business until 1892, when he joined the Meriden

Britannia Company and continued as superintendent of their operations until 1925. The Stevens plant on Community Lake was sold to the Watrous Manufacturing Co. in which Mr. George D. Munson was the chief figure, thus bringing into the silver industry a name that has been prominent ever since. By the way, Seneca Stevens, as a widower, married Dr. Carrie North, Wallingford's first woman physician, who had her office in the ell of my home on the present site of the Post Office.

The date 1898 marked the beginning of the era of the "trusts," combinations of many individual companies in the same line of business into a single large organization, thus effecting great economies in manufacturing and marketing. The leader in this movement was the Meriden Brittania Company which under the name of the International Silver Company merged several of the local silver manufacturers.

Evarts Stevens may well be said to have been born with a silver spoon in his mouth, though not in the accepted sense of having been born to wealth. On the contrary, early in life he learned the business of manufacturing silverware from the bench up, and it was said of him that except for such special trades as die sinking he could take the place of any man in his factories and do a creditable job. He was a modest man; rather shy in disposition who never pushed himself into public view but was promoted because of his devotion to his work whatever it might be, his keen and far ranging intellectual capabilities (he was one of the best read and most knowledgeable man in all fields that I have known) and above all a deeply conscientious regard for the obligations of his position which sprang from the fact that he never forgot his own years at the factory bench. Such character and talent could no more be ignored than a huge oak in a forest of saplings.

The work and influence of Evarts Stevens live in the great plants that dot the adjacent countryside, in the world wide business they supply, and in the thousands they employ. It is highly fitting that his name has been favored in one of our new schools where his character and integrity, his interest in scholarly pursuits, and his deep concern for people can serve as an inspiration for future generations.

It is too bad that the names of Wallace and Simpson are no longer associated with the silver industry, but the Stevens star continues to shine brilliantly in the constellation of the International Silver Co., and thus continues what has become a treasured tradition.

The third member of the triumvirate which dominated the silver industry in Wallingford in its early days was Samuel Simpson. As a youth in 1829 he was apprenticed for a period of several years to learn the trade of pewterer with Charles and Hiram Yale of present Yalesville. Pewter was composed of one-fourth lead and four-fifths tin. The wares were sold mostly by peddlers who traveled by wagon throughout the country. The Yales imported some English workmen who brought with them the formula for Britannia ware, which was susceptible to a much higher polish than pewter.

By 1835, Samuel Simpson had established himself in the business, the Yales retired. Mr. Simpson took up the method of electro-plating and manufacturing with dies rather than moulds, and in 1854 joined with the Wilcoxes of Meriden. When in 1866, the latter decided to build a plant in Meriden, Simpson split with them and formed Simpson Hall Miller Co. and so continued until his death in 1892.

These three men, Wallace, Stevens and Simpson by their industry, intelligence and business acumen were outstanding in establishing the industry on which Wallingford has largely subsisted and grown for over 100 years, so much so that their names have become almost synonymous with those of Wallingford and the silver industry itself. At one time or another all were closely associated with each other in business, making the manner in which partners and businesses were shuffled about in those early days resemble a riotous square dance. It is apparent that competition for the abilities of men, for new alloys, and new methods of manufacture and sales was intense.

Many other names were only a little less prominent in that era. Gurdon Hull, Deacon Almer Hall, Friend Miller, Andrew Andrews and many others contributed their talents and energy to complement those of the leaders.

The old order passeth, and today the silver business constitutes only a relatively minor part of the conglomerates which have either acquired them, or out of which this new type of enterprise has grown. Great oaks grow from little acorns, but there were giants among the men of those days to clear the way.

CHAPTER 25

The Wallingford Disaster

The afternoon of Aug. 9, 1878 in Wallingford was apparently no different from thousands of similar hot, somnolent summer days of the past. Indeed when clouds began to appear in the West, the people welcomed the coming of a shower to cool things off. However, as the sky darkened about six o'clock, the women employed at the Community spoon shop were sent home early, Daniel O'Reilly, who was fishing from a rowboat on the lake, hauled in his line and made for the eastern shore, and men from the factories, having completed the ten hours of work at six o'clock, hurried to get home before the storm broke.

Most of these failed to reach home in time because of the extreme velocity of the storm. Some were killed, some were blown about and injured and all were terrorized by its vicious nature and thoroughly drenched in the downpour which followed. In short, they were caught in the tornado later termed "the Wallingford Disaster." Two huge conflicting masses of unstable air constituting part of a weather front extending all through New England converged from the southwest and northwest over Mt. Tom and Community Lake and formed an updraft at the bottom of which was a rotating vacuum which operated as a huge suction.

Coming over the hill from the west, the tornado toppled the wind mill on the farm of the Wallingford Community and then leveled a small factory near the lake operated by George Grasser, a name still indigenous to the locality. Crossing the lake, the storm found ideal conditions for its worst violence in the level sand plains.

In 1878 the "Plains" was sparcely settled with only a few houses scattered between the lake and Colony St. These were mostly small frame cottages occupied by the Irish families which had come to town in the preceding 25 years. Cutting a swath of some 500 feet across the open expanse, the tornado made short work of the few houses in its path, tearing them literally to pieces.

Reaching Colony St., the storm tore into fragments the frame Catholic Church, leaving nothing but some scattered timbers, a scene vividly shown in a photograph I have. The houses on High St. were a mass of ruins and 11 homes on Wallace Row were entirely destroyed. In the Catholic cemetery headstones were toppled and broken. North of the church on Colony St. the destruction was practically complete as six houses were swept away and 15 people killed. Included in the ruin were the barns which being of lighter construction seemed simply to dissolve, while the animals were carried in some instances many hundred feet. It is a curious fact that not a single horse or cow was killed, and chickens denuded of feathers also survived.

Leaving the Plains the tornado in moving up the Christian St. hill started to "bounce" and when it reached the new North Main Street school sucked off the entire roof and third story, leaving part of the former in a house across the street. At the same time several houses north of the school and several across the street were unroofed. Still standing today are the Munson house, owned by Choate School, the

Miller house next door, and the Parmelee house now owned by Mr. W.A. Reid. This gives a good idea of the width of the tornado's swath as it swept along

In Elm St. two houses behind the Parmelee house were destroyed and a third badly damaged, and many of the magnificent elms planted a century before by Capt. John Atwater were uprooted or split off like match sticks. Indeed many trees were blown down well beyond the immediate path of the tornado as the air moved in with tremendous force toward the vortex of the storm. Thus many of the trees fell in a northerly direction.

The storm continued eastward taking off the roof of the Jones house at the top of the hill and uprooting orchards there and at the Campbell place, now the home of Atty. Fay. The road there was blocked by debris, and access had to be made through the fields, the house badly damaged and the barn gone. Farther east the barn at the Paddock place was lost. Indeed the tornado continued its violent course through the east farms section damaging mostly woodland and orchards at William E. Hall's and Samuel Hopson's farms.

There the tornado met the high barrier of Fowler mountain and the Notches which apparently served to break the suction against the ground, and deflect the vortex upward. The countryside in Durham on the other side of the mountain was littered with debris from the Wallingford houses — broken furniture, mattresses, bedding, and of course, the wreckage from buildings, some as large as 16 foot timbers, one of which dropped into the house of Walter Hart in Durham.

The toll of dead in this catastrophe was 30 of whom half were children including several infants. Thirty-five were badly injured, but recovered, and dozens suffered cuts, bruises and other injuries. The local physicians, Drs. Banks, Harrison, Davis, McGaughey and Atwater, worked valiantly and additional help was summoned by messenger on horseback (no telephones, remember) from North Haven and Meriden.

A tornado is not a good honest storm but a tricky devil that twists and lashes its tail like a snakewhip over the land destroying everything it touches. Nor does it blow in a direct and honorable fashion relying simply on brute force to accomplish its purpose but instead advances with a whirling motion so that at its vortex a vacuum is created. This serves to suck up everything it touches. Thus a building, filled with air, simply explodes, sometimes in all directions, sometimes with the roof flying upward in the surging whirlwind of air. This attack from all sides explains why sometimes a house disappears in pieces, sometimes only the roof is removed, occasionally a part of a structure on the side away from the movement of the storm is destroyed, and trees are felled so that they lie in various directions.

The Wallingford tornado displayed all the tricks of its evil nature. After a slap at the Community farm to show it meant business, it caught Danny O'Reilly rowing toward shore on the lake, picked up the boat with Danny in it and dumped him far up on the bank, half burying him in sand and water. Like the fighting Irishman he was, Danny tried to get up only to be slammed down again. Danny used to say the tornado was the toughest guy he ever tackled and after that he was never afraid of anything during all the later years when he was Wallingford's one man police force, and a terror to evil-doers.

Colony St. was a shamble. Mattie Mooney had been walking along the track toward his house. His body was found in the gutter 415 foot distant. Nearby was the body of Frederick Littlewood and five women of the Mooney family. On Wallace Row, two O'Neil boys were killed, but two other children survived by crouching under the wall of the cellar. Joseph Huldie went upstairs to close a window. He was blown a long distance but survived while his wife and two children downstairs were all killed. From the Toohey house, a 12-year-old boy was blown into a tree, suffering only minor injuries, but Mrs. Toohey was hurled 710 feet into Colony St. Such instances were typical of the carnage on the "Plains."

The freakish nature of the tornado was shown in many strange happenings and miraculous escapes. One man was found with only his collar and shoes still on his body. In one house totally destroyed were nine people. Only one was injured and another blown several hundred feet was not badly hurt. Pat Cline was blown into a tree from which position he saw a cow flying through the air and landing in a cellar from which it emerged with only a broken horn.

On the hill, William M. Hall was returning home from his barn. The barn disappeared and Mr. Hall found himself out in Main St. John Munson saw the tornado coming, grasped a door casing, and found himself next in the cellar, the upper story gone, while four members of his family were found under the timbers unhurt except for bruises.

In the Miller house an oak chair was torn to pieces, but nothing else in the room harmed. Charles Parmelee was in his barn when it took off but managed to escape, got to the house and grasped the door handle but couldn't hold on and was blown away, but not badly hurt. Henry Jones was in his barn when it fell on him, but the pressure on him eased and he extricated himself. As he emerged he saw his horse also walk unharmed out of the ruins. The impulse came over him to shake hands in mutual congratulations!

As already related, the countryside to the East was littered with debris which had been carried up to great heights by the terrific upblast, and gradually spewed out on all sides. A piece of tin roof from the No. Main St. School was picked up in Haddam but most remarkable is the following strange incident.

On the morning after the storm, a certain R. H. Hazard, 2nd of Peacedale, Rhode Island was walking near his home when he picked up the following paper:

"Wallingford, November 24, '76
Received from Mr. P. Cline ten dollars in full account.
James McClarnan"

When Mr. Hazard reached his office he read in the Providence Journal an account of the tornado and the name of John Cline among the injured. Pat Cline's new house was blown to bits with all furniture, clothing, trunks, etc. Not even any of the timbers were left. Word went back to Providence that there had been $50 in the drawer with the receipt and that if found it would be most acceptable. Whereupon the Journal made an appeal to its readers for the lost $50, and as a result the sum of $55 was donated.

In fact donations poured in from many sources and the whole town joined in meeting the catastrophe and its aftermath. One hundred and thirty-eight special constables were sworn in — pay 15 cents an hour — to prevent looting and to control the crowds that came by train and wagon to view the destruction.

Father Hugh Mallon had the distressing task of presiding at one burial service for 29 of his parishioners. I remember him as a thick-set man with a round jovial face. He was also a leader of inflexible determination and unshakable faith as shown by the fact that having lost his church and a large part of his parishioners, in the face of these discouragements and the meagre means of his people, he succeeded in erecting Holy Trinity Church, now

the mother church for several outlying parishes. It is
indeed fitting that this noble man should lie in the
very shadow of the towering monument he left.

There had been tornadoes recorded in
Connecticut before that of 1878, the last in 1787.
That was the only one in which anyone had been
killed, and it would appear the earlier ones were
much less violent or fortunately struck in more
isolated sections. However, since 1878, there has
occurred the tornado in Worcester, Mass. which
apparently was fully the equal of the Wallingford
storm. Such storms are rare in New England whose
rough contours are not conducive to the formation
of this type of wind pattern, yet Mt. Washington has
recorded the highest wind in this hemisphere. But
that was a good honest knockdown and drag out
encounter, not a sneaking, snaky, sucking monster.

CHAPTER 26

Harrison Park

Back in the 1880's, Dr. Henry Harrison was Wallingford's beloved physician, and his wife, Aunt Sarah to Miss Jessie B. Martin whose story this is, was a determined and civic minded woman. Accordingly, she was shocked to hear one day that an enterprising local entrepreneur was negotiating the purchase of the tract of land on North Main Street, west of In Memoriam Cemetery, and planning to open thereon a beer garden and amusement resort for a clamoring public.

Not long before, since the Center Street Cemetery had been outgrown or perhaps I should say had just about reached the point of saturation, the In Memoriam Cemetery Association had been formed and had acquired the beautiful knoll at the end of North Main Street. This was accomplished or accompanied by the sale of lots to a group of prospective users.

According to the social customs of the times and following the usual procedure in the sale of pews in the churches, the best lots and naturally the most expensive went to the top brass or local gentry. Thus you will find the Choates ensconced, or more exactly interred, on the northernmost knoll. Whether this site was chosen so they could enjoy the magnificent view of the Meriden hills, or because it was the most favorable and highest spot for a quick blast-off at the sound of the final trump no one will know.

Not far behind are the Curtises, and separated, as is

fitting in matters of etiquette, by the road, there is the next echelon of honest burghers in professions and trade, the Simpsons, Harrisons, Hubbards, Hales, Wallaces and Leavenworths. Their situation is not so commanding but with the lower slopes on both sides now well filled with solid citizens it is sufficient to give them a sense of satisfaction and well-being.

Be that as it may, as President Arthur Twining Hadley of Yale used to say at the drop of a hat, Mrs. Harrison could not stomach the prospect of a vulgar and noisy beer garden adjacent to her final resting place. She was vaguely familiar with the reputation for raucous goings on of Toelle's at the other end of the street and she wanted none of that within eternal ear shot. So she set to work and since this was well before the day of the telephone, we can speculate that she borrowed her husband's horse and buggy, gowned herself in her best taffeta and bustle and proceeded to call on certain gentlemen of her acquaintance whom she knew to be blessed with an abundance of this world's goods. I mention no names lest I bring a blush of shame to their descendants, because she was rebuffed by one and all.

It may be that these gentlemen thought a little gaiety on the side, so to speak, would lighten the long hours underground, or more likely they saw no good reason to tie up capital which they could double with reasonable frequency   and without income taxes – in a piece of land of no use. They may even have suspected what may well have been the truth that the owner had planted the rumor just to get a good price for a worthless side hill.

Undaunted by her failure, Mrs. Harrison made a decision. She would buy the ground herself and give it to the town for use as a park. She examined her resources, called a family conference, warned her relatives that their inheritances would be reduced, obtained their enthusiastic approval of her action, and Harrison Park was born.

This is not a spacious expanse of rolling hills and

meadows, lakes and forest glades. It is just a steep hillside, edged by barren sand lots and a huge factory complex, but over the years through the loving care of Daniel Reed, it is now a lovely shaded retreat. To be sure it might never have become the dreaded honky-tonk with neon signs and sounds of revelry by night, but today it could well have been nothing but a scrubby hillside, littered with trash.

In Memoriam is quiet at night, and so, thanks to Sarah Harrison, is her park. If a pair of lovers stroll down a path to sit on a bench among the trees, if a ghostly "Dangerous Dan" Reed, trailing clouds of smoke from his pipe and motorcycle exhaust roars noiselessly away home, and if the spirits of the men who died far off return to sigh through the branches of their memorial oaks, these do not disturb her.

CHAPTER 27

The Small Boy of the 90's

The small boy in the 1890's, outside of school hours and during the summer, was left to his own devices. These were varied and numerous and despite the lack of television, mini-cycles, Boy Scouts, summer camp and other improvements in the art of growing up, time rarely hung heavy on his hands.

Hardly had the last snow left the edges of the sidewalks and despite the mud in its wake, marbles and alleys of beautiful colors appeared in the stores, were transferred by purchase or other means to canvas bags and pockets and instantly became a kind of juvenile currency. "Ringers" was the usual type of play. A circle of about a foot in diameter was drawn in the ground and each boy deposited a marble. Lots for first shots were established by rolling an alley to the starting line some 10 feet distant from the circle, the one coming closest getting first shot. Establishment of priority, very important when the circle was well sprinkled with marbles, became immediately a matter of altercation and vociferous argument.

Once established the first shooter knelt down on one knee behind the line, fixed an alley between his thumb and first finger and sent it rolling toward the marbles in the circle. The trick was to have it hopefully hit one or more marbles hard enough to push them out of the circle, and yet leave the alley close enough so that on second round it would be in a favorable position. If the first shooter was successful in knocking any marbles out of the circle, he could continue to shoot from the last position of his alley. The likeness to pool is apparent. All marbles knocked out of the circle became the property of the player, and a good shooter could often clean out the circle before any one succeeding him had a chance to shoot.

In the spring before and especially after school there was almost always a game of "ringers" in progress on the middle sidewalk opposite Moran's Drug Store, and I venture to say that spot marks more quarrels, harsh words, and fist fights than any spot in town, though it is a fair assumption that there was a similar game running downtown.

It is somewhat difficult to establish the exact progression on the calendar of the boy's sport season. March with its high winds was kite season. Boys made their own for the most part, and some were large and intricate but unfortunately were not always successful. Suffice to say that for a week or two it was kite season, and we were busy with sticks, paper, glue, rags for tails and balls of string.

Spring was also the season for tops. These were brilliantly displayed in Pat Wall's store in all colors. A purchase had to be considered carefully, not only as to color to differentiate it from the ordinary, but because of balance, grooving for the winding of the string, the strength of the ring that attached to the finger gave the final snap, and finally the sharpness and solidity of the steel point.

The small boy is nothing if not acquisitive whether it be bird's eggs, butterflies, stamps or money. Tops were the means to acquire money. A gang of boys equipped with tops would waylay every passing man of beneficent mien or otherwise with loud entreaties to "chuck down a cent." If he was disposed to do so, the gang began an immediate assault on the coin with their tops, the idea being to hit it hard enough to put a visible dent in it with the steel point. Here again it is obvious that opportunities for the development of differences of opinion were numerous. Whose top hit the cent first, was the dent a dent or just a scratch and so on until the matter was resolved usually by brute force.

Another game really all season in character was "shinny." This was a forerunner of hockey, and probably a derivation from the ancient game of golf, which in essence is the very simple idea of knocking a ball or stone with a stick into a goal or hole. A shinny was simply a stick with a curved bottom reasonably heavy so the impact on the ball, usually of hard rubber, could send it hurtling through the air or on the ground toward the goal, a line perhaps five feet wide marked by uprights at each end of the field.

For sheer boyish savagery and mayhem no contest could match a good game of shinny. Providing the number of players was reasonably divided between the two sides with age, skill and size taken into consideration, there was no limitation as to participants. Once the ball was put in play in the center, chaos started with one and all trying to get at the ball and hit it toward the opponents' goal. "Shinnies" cracked against shins (an onomatopoetic name for the game), arms, heads and hands, none of which had any protection. If marbles and tops gave rise to provocation and prompt reaction, they were as nothing compared to this Donnybrook.

Behind St. Paul's rectory, then occupied by The Rev. Mr. Wildman, and now the site of the Federal and Loan Building there was in my boyhood an abandoned tennis court. This was in size and flatness an ideal place for "shinny," and it was there as I recall that it was always played. I am left in complete amazement that poor Mr. Wildman, busy with his sermon and doubtless desirous of peace and quiet for his reading, should have permitted this more or less constant storm of battle in his backyard, the air filled with shouts and imprecations. The only explanation I have is the basketful of various liqueur and alcoholic beverage bottles collected from his cellar, and shown to my father and me by his successor, Mr. Greenleaf, accompanied by a shrug of the shoulders and a smile of complete understanding, for both were saintly men and knew that to seek some surcease from the trials and tribulations of life was only human.

CHAPTER 28

East Farm Folks

One hot July afternoon, Uncle Delano and I were sitting in the big barn door of his farm out East, drinking ginger beer. There is no pleasanter or cooler place to sit on a hot muggy day with both big barn doors wide open and the air moving through, bringing with it the scent of the hat just mowed in the field behind it. If it faces the road, as Uncle Delano's door does, the occasional passer-by can stop for a word or two of gossip and news.

So, it was no unusual event when a spring wagon rattled down the hill and drew over into the shade of the barn. High up on the seat sat the driver, a short, spry figure with a white goatee.

"Going to town, Hilary?" inquired uncle Delano. "If you are, I'd be obliged if you'd fetch me a sack of sugar."

"Glad to, Delano. Boy, want a ride in?"

"No," I replied, "I've got my bicycle."

"I'll leave the sack in the barn and collect when I see you — plus interest," and with a flick of his whip he was off, leaving a thick cloud of dust billowing up from the dry road.

As he drove off, a smile spread over Uncle Delano's face and I heard him chuckling. When I looked at him inquiringly, he said:

"He would, too."

"Would what?" I asked.

"Charge me interest. That's my neighbor up the hill, Hilary Jones. He's a constant reminder to me against false pride 'cause the Scripture says, 'Love your neighbor as yourself' so I try hard not to love myself too much." He continued:

"I mind me of the time he had a Guernsey cow, a big milker but a maverick. Cows are funny, all different and with odd notions like all females. Well, this one was possessed to get into my kitchen garden over there, and that lower pasture of Hilary's had a place where the ground was wet, the fence weak, and she could push her way through. I used to have Del lead her up the hill or take her up myself, and I got tired dragging her up."

"So one day when I spotted her in my sweet corn, I said to Del, 'Take a milk pail, draw off a few quarts, take her back and tell Hilary to fix that fence'."

"Well, it warn't more'n a week before there she was again, so this time I told Del to hitch her with one of my heifers and give it a good meal. And this time I told him to get her back through the fence."

"I don't know how many times that summer it happened that one way or another we drew milk off that cow, but one day I saw the vet from town hurryin' up the hill, so I watched for him to come back."

"Somethin' wrong up to Hilary's?" I asked him.

"I don't rightly know, Delano," pondered the vet. "Hilary's got a cow he says is holding up her milk, or perhaps going dry, but I can't find anything wrong."

"Well, Doc," I says, "I don't want you runnin' out here for nothin'. I'll give you a tip. Good fences make good neighbors and bad ones cause trouble for everyone, and you tell Hilary my heifers are unusually good this year."

"I guess the Doc passed the tip along all right 'cause after that Hilary never pastured that cow next to my garden. I thought perhaps he'd mention it sometime and he did indirectly by remarking one day 'I hear your milk production's way up' and 'your heifers look well fed' so finally I came right out and said:

"Hilary, that damned cow o' yours caused me more bother than my whole herd. You didn't do anything about it, so I had to pick a spot on your pocketbook to press on."

"You got well paid for your trouble in milk," says Hilary. "After all, it was my cow."

"And my corn to boot," says I.

"And then what had been rankling him all these years came tumbling out."

"I been spreadin' manure on that field — the one that slopes down to mine next the barn — for twenty years an' the rain just washes it down on your land. My crop is allus scanty — and yours heavy. Is that fair?"

"No," says I, "t'aint fair, and I'll gladly speak to God about it. He made the hill and sent the rain — I didn't."

"Well, that kind o' stumped Hilary. He just grunted and drove off, but left a partin' shot."

"If'n I dropped a dime out o' my pocket, it'd roll down the hill into yours, Delano."

" 'Atween the cows and the manure and a few other little matters, perhaps you see, Clarence, why I keep tight hold on not lovin' myself too much."

" Acourse, I can't say there might not be another side to all this." Fixing me with his blue eyes, he said, "Never take one man's story as gospel till you hear the other's. Hilary's a good farmer, and if he has his rough edges like any Yankee, he'd be a good friend in trouble."

CHAPTER 29

Crime in the 90's

The rash of vandalism, burglaries, petty thefts, drugs, drunkenness, rapes, thuggery, and that delicious phrase "lascivious carriage" reported daily in the press has led me to wonder whether sin is more prevalent in Wallingford today than at the turn of the century. Not that as a boy I was active in the field of crime or exposed to criminal elements in the family, but a small boy gets around, and keeps his eyes and ears open.

Except for that on the highways, Wallingford seems to have been singularly free of murders for some time, but when I was a boy the town was agog with the so-called "shoe box murder." Someone walking in the woods near the present Gaylord Sanatorium came upon a shoe box stuffed with human remains minus the head. They were never identified nor was the crime ever solved.

In retrospect I would have tried to pin it on some shoe clerk who, frustrated by a lady insisting on a number six shoe for a number nine foot, finally went berserk, stabbed the lady with a button hook and in the spirit of the situation, tried to stuff her in toto into the box the shoes came in. Unfortunately, this theory collapsed when research disclosed that shoes used to be shipped in large wooden boxes.

Another crime that greatly upset the town was the defalcation of young Will Trask, who abandoned a lovely wife and two children to abscond to Canada with a substantial bundle of cash belonging to the First

National Bank where he was a teller. This criminal tendency could have been foreseen even by the casual newspaper reader because, not long before, the New Haven Palladium carried an item that "Will Trask and Al Martin were arrested for fishing in Paug Pond." The bank's loss was made good by a well-to-do relative, the matter was hushed up, and the culprit was never prosecuted, but remarried and presumably lived happily in his new environment, thus giving the lie to the aphorism that "crime never pays."

It is my impression that drunkenness was much more prevalent then than now—at least in public. Times were hard, hours of labor 60 a week, and a man couldn't get pleasantly soused at home watching a baseball game on T.V. The saloon and the bottle offered relaxation and a brief release from reality. Also as a result of the depression of the 90's, the town was infested by a stream of tramps who had no place to sleep it off but the street or jail.

Saloons were only steps apart and in fact my grandfather, at one time proprietor of the old Wallingford Hotel, and an uncle both provided oases for the thirsty. I am not too conversant with the prevailing range of prices but a bottle of whisky cost a dollar or less, and a pail of beer or "growler" cost ten or 15 cents. In short, a good snort cost little and more than enough not very much.

Indeed, drunkenness became such an acute problem that it gave rise to violent reactions. Carrie Nation seized her hatchet and began to break up saloons. In a less violent effort, evangelists toured the country, endeavoring to turn the trend toward temperance. Among the most famous of these was Frank Murphy whose emblem was the blue ribbon. My uncle, Judge Hubbard, by no means a total abstainer himself, wearied of decreeing "thirty days in jail" to drunkards and appalled at the misery revealed, was instrumental in bringing Murphy to Wallingford for a series of meetings where many "took the pledge" of total abstinence and for a time at least flaunted the blue ribbon in their buttonholes.

Locally, an organization was formed by the Catholic Church called "The Young Men's Total Abstinence (only from liquor presumably) and Benevolent Society," popularly called "The Tabs." This had an excellent effect in setting a standard for the younger men in the community.

While drinking is perhaps as prevalent today as ever, there doesn't seem to be the same urge to drink to the point of insensibility, and I haven't seen a drunk lying on the sidewalk in years, though this may be due to good police work or my natural aversion to "cocktail lounges."

In my boyhood gambling was included in the normal human sins. Present sophisticated arrangements like the numbers racket and for betting on the horses did not exist, and cards were the mainstay. One outlet for the gambling fever, legitimate on the surface at least, was the "bucket shop." This was a stockbroker's office where the gambler presumably bought stocks on margin. However, instead of actually executing the orders the broker reportedly threw them in a bucket on the basis that the customer was usually wrong in his judgment—as indeed he is still supposed to be today—and if right too often, the broker could fold his tent and steal away. I remember our meat man, Louis Young, was rumored to have lost heavily in this variety of sporting activity.

Of course, there was betting on races at the fairs, and the old shell game which really wasn't gambling at all, but plain fraud on the local yokels. Stud poker flourished but so far as I know there never was a real gambling joint in town complete with roulette, twenty-one and pretty dealers. Today, of course, though it is legally sinful to gamble unless the state can profit from lotteries and parimutuel, and the churches from bingo, and the brokers from commissions, gambling among numerous other human frailties has shed its onus of sin by common participation.

Breaks—excuse me—burglaries—were not common because in a small community it was too easy to pin them on a few individuals. On the other hand, fights, lusty rip-roaring club, bottle and fist fracases, were a frequent occurrence. To break these up and arrest the guilty, Wallingford placed complete confidence in its one policeman, Daniel O'Reilly.

Daniel O'Reilly, Wallingford's one, only, and single police force of the 90's, was about five feet five and perhaps 175 pounds of fighting Irishman, all muscle, bone and sinew, solid as a rock and strong as a bull. I have seen him push, pull and drag a man seemingly twice his size up Center St. hill and literally throw him into the jail in the rear of the present town hall — excuse me, City Hall.

That jail, by the way, was no bed of roses, either as to comfort or smell, but in those unregenerate days if a man was incarcerated it was considered to be his own fault, not that of society, and if he didn't like it, he could stay out of it in the future. In breaking up a fight, Danny was not prone to inform the participants of their rights to advice of counsel, but waded in with both fists and a blackjack, at which he was very adept, to settle the dispute, not in one way or another, but just his way.

Danny was famous all over the state for his prowess. He was fearless and neither size or numbers fazed him. He was so tough that even the tornado of 1878 which sucked him and his boat out of Community Lake and deposited them well up toward the Catholic Church failed to harm him or disturb his imperturbability. So Danny didn't relish the job of bringing to court a Miss Tillie Anderson and her young lady seminarians.

Miss Anderson, a not unattractive middle-aged faded blonde, conducted a residence for young ladies on the Yalesville Rd. In good old English, the name for it would have been brothel, but it would do the stately three-story country house less than justice to call it by that name with its connotations of a filthy, back-alley

city location. Tillie's place was always referred to by
that good old Victorian semanticism as "a house of
ill-fame," invariably in hushed tones.

About once a year Tillie and her brood of chicks —
if I may descend to levity — was rounded up by the
efficient Officer O'Reilly and escorted down to court.
Unfortunately, on such occasions we boys were
rigorously excluded from our usual front seat in the
courtroom so I can't supply a firsthand account of the
proceedings. My guess is that Tillie pleaded guilty, paid
the fine out of her capacious and well-lined pocket,
returned to her establishment with her young ladies, and
promptly reopened for business as usual.

Whether this whole procedure was designed to
discourage sin by raising the cost or was regarded merely
as a regular source of annual revenue for the police
court is a moot matter. The fact remains that by mutual
understanding and consent, Tillie was disturbed only
once a year and certainly no gentlemen callers were
brought in, which leads me to believe that there must
have been some skulduggery somewhere.

In the days of equine transportation, it used to be
said that any horse from Ingraham's or Booth's stables,
given his head, would proceed entirely on his own to the
leafy shadows of Tillie's back yard. This habit was
doubtless fostered by traveling salesmen, notoriously lax
in morals, and not to any local trade. Later, when the
electric trolley cars took over, it was reported that a
blush mantled the fair cheek of Miss Yale whenever she
rode past on the way to her teaching duties in Yalesville.
But these tales are doubtless apocryphal.

In the related field of rapes and similar
peccadilloes, the small boy of the 90's was too naive
even to identify the nature of the crime. We didn't have
the advantages of today's television, newspapers, movie
ads, paperbacks and especially the sex education offered
by the churches. That is not to say we were entirely
oblivious to the fascinations of sex in such instance as
that previously described. I presume rapes, official and

unofficial, were certainly as prevalent then as now, since human nature, if it changes at all, changes little in a mere seven decades. Anyway, my memory is a blank in this interesting category of crime, and indeed, it seems rare today. Why should anyone snatch a crust of bread when a full table-de-hostess dinner can be had for the asking?

In concluding this discussion, my theory on sin is that since little progress seems to have been made in persuading people to fight it, the way to eliminate it is to join it. For instance, most people, as I will demonstrate in a later article, are thieves, so stealing certainly is no longer culpable. Coveting of one's neighbor's ox or his ass has fallen off greatly, and even emulation of King David's affair with Bathsheba is no longer common hereabouts. Today when the seventh commandment is more honored in the breach — if I may use the word — than in the observance, this particular sin seems to have been eliminated by popular disregard. Why cannot the seven deadly sins and the three extra of the ten commandments gradually be abolished in this manner?

However, this would remove the necessity for churches and I enjoy a good sermon, no matter how ineffectual it may be, more than almost anything else. So put me down with Calvin Coolidge as against sin — in Wallingford especially.

CHAPTER 30

The Country School

Whenever I happen to pass Wall's or Rose's parking lots and see the dozens of school buses my mind reverts to my father-in-law. He was born in 1857 on a small farm some five miles from a village in New Hampshire. He and his six brothers walked to the school in the village and back in good weather and bad. Anyone who has lived through a New Hampshire winter with its ever present snow and ice and low temperatures can perhaps appreciate the hardship and even danger involved in such a harsh routine.

Not that I immediately think that those were the good old days when children were brought up to face the realities of life at an early age because in fact the hardships of the era were such as to fill the cemeteries with children's graves. They did result in those that lived being toughened, and, in this case, all survived to become dentists, physicians, musicians and teachers.

Furthermore, before studying for these professions, they were expected to serve out the time until their 21st birthday in labor on the farm for their father. After that they were free to start their careers with little, if any, help from home. Indeed the annual cash income of the family was about $100, and what few necessities and luxuries that could not be raised or made on the farm were obtained by barter.

Reference has been made in preceding columns to the New England genius for invention forced by the necessities of finding solutions to the problems of eking out an existence in the brutal environment. Thus it was that to while away the long winter evenings, the boys formed an orchestra, and the father made various musical instruments, including a violin with which one of them in later life won the Henry Ford contest for old-time fiddling.

Wallingford a hundred years ago was kinder to its children and by the dispersal of its district schools probably limited the walking distance to perhaps two miles which was far enough in rain, snow and ice. The school system in town in the '90's, as I remember, consisted of the No. Main St. School with the grades on the lower floors and the High School on the third, the Colony St. School, the old So. Main St. School on the site now occupied by the Bartek residence, the Simpson School and the newly-built Whittlesey Ave. School.

Outside town in the farming districts, there were the normal one room country schoolhouses, strategically placed to serve as conveniently as possible the children in the various districts. The one with which I am most familiar was the East Farms School. The site of this schoolhouse is now beneath the waters of MacKenzie Reservoir, but it lay just East of the viaduct which bisects the lake on the corner of Scard and Whirlwind Hill Roads, and on the very bank of Muddy, or if you prefer the polished up version, Pine River. The schoolhouse was moved to Williams Road and continues its usefulness as a residence.

There my mother went to school with her brothers and sisters, my mother-in-law and many old friends. Men prominent in town affairs like Delavan Ives Sr., Linus Hall and the Youngs were pupils there. The teacher for many years was Miss Mary Martin who, for a stipend of some $300 per year, struggled with the education and even more difficult discipline of children from six to 14 years old, some of the older boys outweighing her by a wide margin. Indeed one estimable Wallingford lady, now gone, who was especially mischievous in her youth, used to tell me how Miss Martin in exasperation seized her by the shoulders and bounced her up and down in her seat until she "saw stars."

The old North Farms schoolhouse on Barnes Rd. between Leigus Rd. and I-91 was sold by the town and converted into an attractive residence, as was the west side district school on Parker Farms Rd. I believe there was a schoolhouse in the Pond Hill district, but I am unable to pinpoint its location. Another that has disappeared was located on Old Durham Rd. on the north side of the curve just beyond the junction with Williams Rd. The foundation stones are still scattered on the site.

The disappearance of Wallingford's district schools or their conversion so as to make them unrecognizable is so general throughout Connecticut that it is difficult to find today an example remaining in all its pristine simplicity. Thus we are fortunate that Northford has preserved the schoolhouse which used to stand some miles South of the village on present Route 22. Several years ago this was moved to Northford center and relocated just north of the library. It is a one-room country schoolhouse at its best in the sense of being plain and stark and lacks only the sanitary facilities which were normally situated some distance away modestly and discretely shaded by bushes or small trees. The date on the building is 1805, and I have a strong sentimental attachment to it because my grandmother, Eliza Bartholomew, taught there about 1830. A photograph of the schoolhouse on its original lot is pictured here.

Those interested in such preservations of an earlier era in education may wish to examine an old schoolhouse that has been recently removed from the crest of Parmelee Hill Rd. in Durham to North Guilford where at present it is located on Wilburs Lane near the churches on the hill. This building is most unusual, if indeed not unique for a schoolhouse, because it has a

vaulted ceiling. The beams were hand fashioned in a graceful curve which must have given the school room a very lovely, and certainly a highly distinctive appearance, and in addition perhaps, as a touch which all school teachers would appreciate, improved ventilation.

The district schoolhouse was a reflection of its era in the hard, toilsome and flinty character of the environment both physically and socially. Merely going to school and back home in bad weather presented constant problems of wet clothing and wet feet. Dependence on a wood stove in winter meant a cold room at first, followed by a condition in which those nearer the stove roasted if those farther away were to be kept from freezing. The teacher not only suffered the same physical hardships, but had to be a mother to the young children, act as father in the discipline of the older ones, and in the meantime teach all the grades from primary arithmetic to algebra, from ABC's to English literature. Naturally, such education was simple, basic and direct — enough arithmetic to add and subtract for ordinary transactions, geography of the states and capitols and the continents and ability to write without misspelling too many words.

Progress in education in the last 100 years has perforce essentially matched the progress in technology. What has been to some extent lost is the close human touch between teacher, pupil and parent, and the toughening rough and tumble of all ages in the close proximity of the schoolhouse yard.

CHAPTER 31

The Missing Denture

A dentist's office, furnished with easy chairs and movie magazines, and drenched in soft music to soothe the irritated nerves, is usually a place where privacy is secure. Such indeed were usually the parlors of Dr. Craig in the Masonic Building and Dr. Barker in the Simpson Block where for some half century these two professional men ministered to those people in Wallingford who had their natural teeth and to those less fortunate who preferred the futile deceit of artificiality to the alternative of "gumming it."

So it was that one winter morning many years ago I was stretched out on Dr. Barker's chair like a man on a rack, equipped with bib and tucker and a rubber dam in my mouth while he plumbed carefully with his drill for the farthest extremity of a caries in one of my molars, when we heard the office door open, followed by the patter of feet and then a high pitched cackle.

"Good morning, Doctor. Got someone in the chair?"

A small, plump, rosy faced figure scuttled in and peeked around my back.

"Oh, it's you, Clarence. Something the matter?" She tried to look into my mouth, but was baffled by the dam and Dr. Barker's hand which together left little room for external observation. I wanted to tell her I was just there enjoying the sunset and waiting calmly for death.

"Hope it doesn't hurt," she continued. "Don't you want to buy two tickets for the Fireman's Ball? They cost a dollar apiece, but," her voice dropped to a conspiratorial whisper, "you can have these for $1.75."

Dr. Barker straightened up with the patience and self control of long experience, reached for his wallet and said,

"O.K., Mena, you win. Where did you pick them up?" This was a sly reference to Mena's adeptness in acquiring any loose articles. She replied,

"From Bobbie Hyatt."

— — — — — — — — — —

At this point, it seems advisable, if not indeed necessary to justify your continuing interest, to sketch in lightly a bit of background about our heroine. Mena Bates, although a maiden lady, was seldom called Miss except perhaps by some itinerant salesman. In the village of Wallingford as a whole or individually she was always addressed directly as Mena. If referred to in the third person, it was always monosyllabically as Menabates. She was, I think, under five feet in height and plump; in mentality, a curious combination of childish naivete, of curiosity, and cunning. One was never sure whether to treat her as a child or as one full of guile.

Her dress could have come from a Lilliputian fashion magazine. In winter a long coat, probably adopted from the wardrobe of some friendly neighbor's daughter, swept the ground, and in real cold weather was supplemented by a tippet several feet long which she wound several times around her neck, passed under her arms, and tied in a knot at the back. On her head she wore a bonnet which resembled that of an organ grinder's monkey, a simile which probably has little recognition today.

Mena's finances were very limited, consisting chiefly of an inherited house on So. Main St. which she rented, retaining only a room for herself. A wealthy neighbor supplied a substantial check at Christmas, and others just "looked out" for her. Her daily wants were supplied from her occupation which was not surprising if you think about it for it was as reporter for an out-of-town paper. For this service she received a small stipend for each item deemed sufficiently newsworthy to be accepted. With this incentive she was constantly scurrying around town.

Her status as a reporter gave Mena the right of entrance to all public affairs, and indeed Mena did not always distinguish between public and private events, leading occasionally to the submitting of items which if published might well have led to libel or other even more unfortunate denouements. The most important aspect of this reportorial status was that it gave Mena access without charge to church suppers of all denominations, to theatrical productions, balls, sleigh rides and parties large and small.

Thus, Mena was able to eat well reasonably often, and to lead a generally gay life. Indeed, as a purveyor of the latest happenings, intentions and plain gossip, she was a welcome and accepted figure in the life of the community. One of her most cherished privileges was that of being a once-a-week guest of Mr. and Mrs. Robert Hyatt at dinner at St. George's Inn, the former Beach mansion which they operated as lessees from the Choate School.

We left our heroine, Miss Mena Bates, in the dentist's office arranging the sale at a cut price of two tickets to the Firemen's Ball, but called upon to prove there was nothing illicit in her possession of the pasteboards. One would think Mena would have resented such an implied slur on her integrity and freedom from deceit or petty larceny, but in this case there was no need for violent protestations of her honesty.

One winter afternoon, Robert Hyatt having discharged for the nonce his duties as host at St. George's, slipped into a seat on the aisle at Wilkinsons'

Emporium of the Theatrical Arts, and prepared for a brief period of relaxation by removing his dental bridge in order to dislodge a seed from a very tasty fig pudding of Mrs. Hyatt's expert concoction. As he held the teeth in his hand ready for reinstatement in any emergency of unexpected greetings from a friend, he watched the antics of Donald Duck on the screen. For some reason these did not appeal to his English sense of humor, and gradually his eyes closed and he slept. Awakening with a start, a glance at the clock showed he was long past due back at the Inn, so grabbing his coat he hastily departed.

_ _ _ _ _ _ _ _ _

Late that same afternoon, Mena Bates, having successfully garnered six items about projected Valentine parties and other activities of Wallingford's elite, entered Wilkinson's with the pleasurable anticipation of watching the latest episode in the "Perils of Pauline" followed by her weekly luxurious dinner at the Inn, her euphoria whetted to a state of almost beatific bliss by the fact that neither involved any out-of-pocket expense. As she peeled off her tippet it slipped to the floor and stooping to pick it up her hand came in contact with a hard object. Anything loose was worth inspection from Mena's practical viewpoint, so she picked it up only to find it was an apparently dilapidated piece of dentistry. Nevertheless she slipped it in her pocket.

The possibility of turning her find in at the office may have occurred to Mena, but long experience had taught her that umbrellas, gloves and especially money turned over to a third person rarely resulted in ultimate possession to the finder. So to Mena treasure-trove was finders keepers. So after watching Pauline barely escape decapitation by a steam engine, she adjourned to the Inn. There after eating all she could ingest without spilling over, she happened to remember the find in her coat pocket, so when Mr. Hyatt was with true British gentility helping her into her coat, she remarked:

"See what I found in Wilkinson's?"

Bobbie took one look at the denture, clapped his hand to his mouth and exclaimed:

"My God, those are my teeth."

"So," Mena concluded in a voice like thorns crackling under a pot, "that's how I got the tickets. Bobbie was so pleased to get his teeth back he gave them to me.

"Have a good time, Doctor. I'll be there and if you want a dance, you'd better ask me now."

CHAPTER 32

Aunt Sarah's

On a pleasant summer afternoon, first looking out the window to the west to make sure no thunder shower was impending, my mother was likely to say, "It's so nice, Clarence, I think we'll drive up to see Aunt Sarah. Besides, Mr. Hale (I never heard my mother address my father or refer to him by his first name and I sometimes wonder how I ever happened) suggested that Nellie needs some exercise."

Nellie was our mare. It was mentioned, probably by the seller, that Nellie had once stepped out a smart 2.20 but possibly because of adding some weight in her middle years and becoming more sedate, I was never able to get up to more than a slow jog trot from which she soon lapsed into a diminuendo until she was back in her usual walk. But Nellie was a gentle beast and I never saw her really aroused except on one occasion.

She was stabled at Mr. Hall's on Elm St. and having been sent to fetch her I was driving west on Center St. by the Town Hall when a circus parade, led by a huge lumbering elephant appeared over the brow of the hill. Nellie took one look at this strange behemoth, turned in her tracks, almost upsetting the carriage, and made for her stable at her former racing speed. I calmed her down eventually and made home by way of Ward St. However, after that she couldn't deceive me as to her ability to hold her own with horses in Ingraham's, Morse's or Booth's racing stables.

I must say we made a handsome sight as we drove up Main St. in our red buggy with rubber tired wheels. Of course, we could hardly be compared with Mr. Gurdon Hull's high stepping pair for which it was rumored he had paid the eye-opening sum of three hundred dollars. We usually went to the end of Main St., turned by the old Royce house where the Washington elm had stood for some 200 years and been blown down in 1896, and then over dusty country roads to Aunt Sarah's.

Her farm was on the flatlands near the reservoir which Simpson, Hall, Miller had built to maintain power for their factory downtown. These beautiful acres had been acquired by a perspicacious member of the Ives family soon after they were bought from the Indians in 1669 as part of the town. Uncle Walter, who had married my mother's aunt, Sarah Bartholomew, had been dead for some time, and Aunt Sarah ran the farm with the help of a young man named Fred McGuire. And finally I am getting around to my story.

When we drove in at the farm, Aunt Sarah would usually appear and with her two unmarried daughters, Victorine and Georgene. Aunt Sarah was a vigorous old lady with her hair drawn tightly back and tied in a bun. Victorine, the older of the girls by 10 years, was a rather tall, scrawny, hatchet faced New Englander, but Georgene or "Gene" as she was called was somewhat attractive in a buxom way with a pleasant smile. It can be imagined that life on a farm in those days was a tiresome, drab existence, and as the years wore on, the girls had acquired a tired and lacklustre appearance.

The ladies, of course, went in the house to talk while I accompanied Fred on his chores, feeding the stock, greasing the harness, and sometimes haying in the big field south of the house. I can still remember how good that cold ginger beer tasted on a hot July day when Cousin Gene brought us a big pitcher full.

Well, as time went on, I noticed Fred seemed preoccupied and sometimes even morose instead of his

usual jolly self, and one day when we went up to Aunt
Sarah's, Fred wasn't there. They told me he had been
offered a good job in the factory and had decided to
take it.

That evening I heard my mother in the next room
with my father mention Fred's name and Cousin Gene's
so I pricked up my ears. "Aunt Sarah," my mother said,
"just wouldn't have it."

"I don't know why not," replied my father. "I
never heard anything against him and a lot for him. He
certainly ran the farm well. And Gene's no prize
package either at her age."

"But, Mr. Hale," objected my mother, "he's Irish."

"And," burst out my father, "St. Patrick was an
Englishman, the Queen of England is German, Jesus
Christ was a Jew, and everybody's grandfather was a
monkey."

With this astonishing and to me utterly irrelevant
remark my father resumed reading the evening paper.

Aunt Sarah's comfortable old farm house has
disappeared, burned to the ground many years ago, and
only the stump remains of the great sycamore that used
to shade the house and yard on the south. I understand
the broad acres, as lush today with corn as ever, have
been purchased as the site for a new Catholic high
school. On the roster in the years to come may well be a
representation of McGuires, but there will be no boys
and girls with the Ives and Bartholomew blood coursing
in their veins for that branch has withered away and
died.

CHAPTER 33

Town and Gown

Two recent events in juxtaposition have served to point up a relationship of such long standing and acceptance that its importance tends to be overlooked. The first was the composition or adjustment between the tax authorities of Wallingford and the Choate School with regard to certain residential properties belonging to the school. The second was the use of the school grounds and Winter Exercise Building in our Tercentenary celebration.

The growth of the school in the past 75 years has been so gradual and unobtrusive that it is difficult for us "townies" to realize it has become a national institution with international relations. Choate has never forced itself on the town as have some schools and many colleges which by reason of original situation sprout up in the midst of a community and threaten to tear it apart. Choate has minded its own business very effectively, I might say, and left Wallingford to do the same, not in any spirit of snobbery or exclusiveness but purely on the basis that it had a job to do, and wanted to put its mind on its work. Yet it has always been generous in its thought and in its acts, and taken altogether these are the factors that make up a good neighbor.

It is time, I think, that Wallingford be reminded of just how good a neighbor Choate has been over what is now approaching a century of living close to each other.

Of course, in the early days the presence of the school was hardly noticeable, a few boys seen occasionally on the streets, the masters mingling in the social life of the town, and on the outskirts some buildings for the most part hardly distinguishable from the local scene.

But Choate grew in numbers under the driving energy of Dr. George St. John, and the few dozen became a few hundred. The neighborhood began to take shape as a school entity with the addition of a lovely chapel and impressive Georgian-style brick buildings for library and science and athletics. Choate was silently but forcefully setting up standards of beauty and utility for the community to look up to and hopefully to try to equal.

Choate as an educational institution has a reputation second to none, and in making its advantages available to local youth, it has performed a great and continuing service to the town. The picture of the school in its early days shown in Tercentenary publications reveals the fact that local boys made up some 60 per cent of the whole school. I was among them, and I have never ceased to be grateful that when so young I had the advantages of superior teaching and an environment which nurtured the opening up of a boy's mind. Through its many decades since, hundreds of local boys have continued to enjoy the constantly increasing facilities of the school, and have been graduated to go on to our best colleges and into distinguished and constructive careers.

Choate has always kept its doors open, not only for our boys, but for all citizens who wished to accept their constant stream of invitations to the public to attend free many concerts and lectures by distinguished artists and public men, the school plays, and the athletic contests on football field, diamond, and track.

Not only have members of the faculty circulated socially in town and in many instances become firm and lifelong friends, some at least have given of their talents and time to town affairs. Who can forget the contribution of the Ayres family, or Bill Shute, and very likely others I may unintentionally omit?

I doubt if many know and few remember that during the awful period of the great depression in the early 1930's Choate, which then had a large dairy herd, contributed gratis thousands of quarts of milk to the children of Wallingford.

My son reminds me that when he was at Choate during those troubled times, the boys adopted an austerity diet as a result of which Choate, hard pressed as it was itself, contributed food, and each Saturday a Choate truck manned by the boys distributed baskets of provisions to the distressed families of Wallingford. There must be many of our citizens who as children had the benefit of having their bellies filled at least once a week through the humanity of Choate.

The statement is sometimes made that Choate doesn't pay taxes. That of course is not true. They do pay taxes on what is agreed to be taxable property. Of course, Choate sends very few of its family to the public schools, the cost of which constitutes some 60 per cent of the Town's budget. What Choate pays in money covers its taxable legal responsibilities, but what Choate contributes to the community in other ways is beyond price.

For now we are to have the Mellon Arts Center with its treasures, and a large hall for concerts and plays. Our streets are to be brightened by girls from Rosemary Hall. And in all that part of town which Choate touches, there is always the loveliness of the landscape developed by the genius of John Ed Wilfong.

But what of town and gown? Where are the incursions of ebullient youth from the school into the town with damage to property and irritation of feelings? Where the friction bursting into fiery fisticuffs over the love of some local damsel? Where the meetings between gangs of Choaties and townies with the police called to break it up? I did read some time ago of a Choate boy being roughed up by some rowdies for no ostensible reason. Perhaps he wore his hair short and spoke English! Certainly it is a fact that for three-quarters of a century relations between Choate boys and the community have been harmonious, courteous and cordial, as Oliver Foote would testify.

So, when the chimes of the Choate chapel ring sweetly over the town to mark the passing of the hours, let us all remember that Choate as a good neighbor stands ready to discuss and bring to an amicable and equitable settlement any differences that may arise, and is ready when called upon to extend a generous hand in the loan of its facilities in every good work the town may undertake.

CHAPTER 34

Oliver Foote

The late Oliver D. Foote was one of the most delightful and colorful personalities that have enriched the life of Wallingford during the current century. He came here from Bridgeport about 1900, a period I remember because when we boys were skylarking in his store we were reproved as "not acting like gentlemen." This reproof in itself was highly characteristic and he was always insistent on the maintenance of decorum and good behavior in his establishment.

With the opening of his "parlor" — what a lovely Victorian euphemism — Wallingford was to have an institution where one not only partook of the best ice cream sodas and candy that could be produced, but participated in a keen contest of wits, recounting of anecdotes, and inevitably and always bawdy but never dirty stories. Above all else, O. D. loved a good story and it made no difference whether he himself was the butt of it or not. And one of his favorites was the following:

Shortly after his arrival in Wallingford, he thought it would be a good idea to familiarize himself with the town and its environs. In a natural sequence of such tours, one fine morning he took the trolley car at the station with the intention of seeing the Masonic Home and the west side, and then walking back to his store on Center St.

As he boarded the trolley car, he noted a number

of ladies on their way to shop in Meriden, took a seat on
the front seat by the motorman, and was soon rattling
down Quinnipiac St. with the motorman banging on his
foot gong at the cross streets. There was plenty to see,
the Wallace factories, the river, the Watrous
Manufacturing Co. and the broad sweep of Community
Lake with Paradise Island and some early picnickers.

Suddenly, O. D. realized that he must have passed
the Masonic Home, that the car was now bouncing along
at the furious rate of 15 or 20 miles an hour, and that
the walk back was going to be longer than intended.
Furthermore, the town had stopped with only an
occasional farm house back in the fields.

At first the motorman, certain that none of his
passengers would want to get off before Yalesville, and
with his attention focused on his forward progress with
its possibility of a stray dog or cow, gave no need to O.
D.'s request that the speeding vehicle be stopped in its
wild career so he could be let off. By that time, they
were passing Wooding's Pond so O. D. tugged at the
motorman's coat, and indicated he wanted to get off.
The motorman gave O. D. a surprised look, shrugged his
shoulders, revolved the breakwheel and brought the car
to a stop in front of a large country house — the only
one in fact on that long stretch of flat road.

O. D. thanked him, jumped off the car, waved
genially to the ladies, gave a glance at the quiet,
shuttered house, and turned his steps toward town. It
was a long, long time before O. D., who was completely
ignorant of the variety and location of the amusements
available in his new abode, found out why he was
shunned by the ladies, young and old, of Wallingford,
for word had spread quickly through the community
that that young Mr. Foote, who had just opened an ice
cream parlor, had been observed visiting Miss Tillie
Anderson's establishment, not discreetly in the evening
hours which might have been overlooked in a gay young
blade, but in broad daylight — morning no less — and he

had even thumbed his nose at the ladies when he got off the trolley.

O. D. was not oɪ commanding stature nor did he have the roving eye and the devil-may-care look usually associated with a dissolute rake with women, so as he leaned over his soda bar to recount this tale in all its graphic details, the episode took on such an aspect of absurdity as to make the room resound with guffaws of laughter.

But if indeed Tillie — and this is the last time she will be honored by mention — and her bevy of beautiful blondes had entered his parlor to regale themselves on banana splits, they would have been treated with punctilious courtesy for O. D. was a bred-in-the-bone gentleman.

CHAPTER 35

The Interloper

Deacon Eliakim Peck sat at his desk in the library of his ancestral home on Main St. The mellow October sun flooding into the room was reflected from the polished tables on the faces of the portraits that lined the walls above the fireplace and bookcases. The Deacon always derived a deep sense of satisfaction from sitting back in his chair and letting his eyes roam over these evidences of the nobility of his heritage.

Occasionally, however, he felt a twinge of unease, imagining that the eyes of the portraits regarded him with gentle reproach, and the reasons were self evident to him. For the truth of the matter was that Deacon Peck while of highly estimable character was undistinguished in any of the various fields of arms, theology, government or law in which his forbears had been pre-eminent.

The other reason for his disquietude was that he had no son to carry on the family name, and hopefully its traditions of high distinction. His only child was a daughter, Cynthia, now 22 years old and at home after graduation from college the previous June. That Cynthia was lovely in person and engagingly intelligent were compensations, to be sure, but there remained a persistent sense of inadequacy.

Hearing the sound of wood being thrown to the ground he rose from his desk and looked out the window. In the driveway of the house across the street a wagon load of fireplace wood was being emptied and stacked. Busily occupied at the job was a tall, well built young man with curly blond hair and talking to him as opportunity afforded was his daughter. At the sight the Deacon felt a surge of sharp uneasiness, almost resentment. He knew that in high school Cynthia had rather liked the boy, a "Polack" as the Deacon termed him, named Tad Mietkiewicz, not that the Deacon could or would even try to pronounce the name. The Deacon had assumed that four years of college would create the natural social gulf, and he was startled to see that his unacknowledged strategy had failed.

Actually, the Deacon had nothing against the young fellow. On the contrary his family had operated a good farm several miles from town for half a century, the grandfather having come to Connecticut from the West. Young Tad, he understood, had attended a neighboring state agricultural college. It was just that the Deacon harbored the old New England distrust of anything foreign.

As the Deacon observed the scene across the street, it occurred to him that he would need wood for his fireplace in the coming winter. His brother had sold his place from which the Deacon had previously derived his supply as a fraternal gesture, so it would be necessary to get it elsewhere. He walked to the door and called to Cynthia, subconsciously intending to break off the conversation for an ostensibly good reason.

"What is it, Dad?" she inquired as she approached.

"I shall need some fireplace wood," said the Deacon. "Do you think Tad would bring me a load? Tell him I want a cord in two foot lengths of solid hard wood with a sprinkling of smaller pieces for kindling. And ask the price."

The Deacon never took chances of a price lagging behind a deal, especially with foreigners.

"All right, Dad," replied Cynrhia. "I'll ask him."

Whereupon she recrossed the street and resumed an animated conversation with Tad which the Deacon noted from his vantage point seemed far longer than necessitated by merely ordering the wood. However, he soon heard the wagon going away and Cynthia entered to tell him it was all arranged, the price was $16 a cord, and the wood would be delivered later in the week.

Accordingly several days after Tad appeared with the wood and under the Deacon's instructions, delivered personally both to be sure they were carried out correctly, that is the wood to be stacked against the house by the kitchen, and to prevent a resumption of the conversation he had seen with such vague and unrecognized uneasiness. He had intended to pay Tad for the wood, but before he realized the fact, Tad had left feeling perhaps a little embarrassed to disturb the Deacon.

Looking over the stacked wood, the Deacon was pleased with the large hunks of long burning oak and hickory, but suddenly it occurred to him that there was not as much wood in the stack as he had expected for a cord. Never one to overlook the possibility of getting the short end of a purchase, the Deacon went to the closet and emerged with a yard stick. From school days he remembered a cord should be four feet wide, four feet high and eight feet long — one hundred and twenty-eight cubic feet. He soon determined that this stack was about six feet high and short of ten feet long and, of course, two feet wide. Mentally, the Deacon figured the cubic content as short of one hundred and twenty — perhaps even a couple of feet less.

Hurriedly, he went to his library, consulted the dictionary under "cord" and slammed it shut. His innate xenophobia, whose existence under normal circumstances he would have refused to admit, burst out in an imprecation. "Damned foreigners! They'll cheat you every time."

To make sure, he went out again, stacked the logs as evenly as possible, measured with great care, and computing the results on paper came up with one hundred eighteen and five eighths cubic feet. Passing Cynthia in the kitchen, the Deacon said, "Please have that young man of yours stop in the next time he's in town."

Something in the tone of his voice caused Cynthia to glance at him, perplexed, and she replied, "He's hardly that, but what's the matter?"

The Deacon was not a man of violent temper, but merely mildly astigmatic from his New England heritage, and besides he had the feeling of having an ace in the hole so he said simply, "Oh, he didn't come in to get paid," and continued on into the library.

Accordingly, he was loaded for bear, as the expression goes, when several days later Cynthia appeared at the library door with Tad in tow. The Deacon rose from his chair at the desk, gestured to Tad to sit down and made his carefully considered gambit.

"That is very nice wood you brought, Tad, but it appears to be a little short of the cord I ordered."

Slowly, as the significance of the words sank in, a blush rose on Tad's face to the roots of his blond hair.

"Deacon — sir — " he stuttered, then collected himself while Cynthia standing by the door exclaimed, "Father, how could you say such a thing!"

"Are you implying, sir," continued Tad, "that I gave you short measure?"

The Deacon in his turn, somewhat taken aback by Tad's obvious astonishment as well as Cynthia's outburst, adopted a more placating tone.

"Well, Tad, I have always understood a cord of wood should contain one hundred and twenty-eight cubic feet. I measured that you brought and it seems to be less than one hundred twenty."

Slowly a smile spread across Tad's face and pulling at his wallet he extracted a somewhat dog-eared paper.

"I guess, Deacon, you don't happen to be informed on the peculiarities of wood measure. If you will glance at this official bulletin of the Dept. of Agriculture you can see that the standard cord of one hundred and twenty-eight feet is applicable to four foot logs, but when the wood is cut in shorter lengths, it fits closer together, so you get less cubic feet but actually the same amount of usable wood."

Tad consulted the paper.

"Yes, here is the table. For two foot lengths one hundred and ten feet cubic feet shall constitute one cord."

Completely discomfitured, the Deacon reached mechanically for the paper but he knew he was caught in an embarrassing situation and did so only to hide his confusion. To say he was taken aback would be to describe his feelings too mildly. He was completely flabbergasted. To make matters worse his ace in the hole had turned out to be a deuce. He had only to glance at Cynthia's amused expression to realize he was not only now on the defensive, but in a weak strategic position.

However, the Deacon was much too experienced a man to lose his aplomb completely, and gazing at the paper, he said, "You are quite right. It's completely logical but it never occurred to me and hitherto my brother has supplied my wood gratis. I'm sorry if I was under the wrong impression."

"That's all right, Deacon," said Tad, anxious to have the breach healed as quickly as possible. "I certainly wouldn't cheat anybody," and with an involuntary glance at Cynthia, "let alone you."

"Yes, father," put in Cynthia, "you ought to be sorry. I think we all ought to have a glass of sherry and declare peace."

The Deacon winced because she always called him Dad except when she was angry at him.

Cynthia went to the cupboard, pushed aside the decanter of California wine, and reaching inside drew out the Deacon's pet and rarely produced bottle of Bristol cream. As she poured the dark rich liquid into the glasses she gave Tad a sidelong glance accompanied by the suggestion of a wink, completely lost on her father who was engaged in writing out the check.

In the meantime, Tad's eyes had settled on the portrait of an officer in the Continental Army and he rose and walked over to examine it more closely.

"May I ask, Deacon, whose portrait this is?" he inquired.

At once the Deacon felt his feet touch terra firma. The family portraits were the apples of his eye.

"That, Tad, is Major Theophilus Peck. He went to Quebec with Arnold and fell at the battle of White Plains. He was an aide to Washington and it's through him I hold membership in the Society of the Cincinnati."

Now that the Deacon was launched, he had no intention of being diverted.

"The primitive over the bookcase is of William Peck, an associate of Eaton and Davenport in the founding of New Haven. This one is Ezekiel Peck, a sea captain and privateer in the War of 1812. The gentleman in robes is my grandfather, Judge Epaminondas Peck of the state Supreme Court, and the one over the cupboard is his father, Senator Eliphalet Peck. You will notice it is a tradition in the Peck family to use a long first name to balance the short last one."

The Deacon returned to his chair confident that the young man had been duly impressed.

"It's possible," mused Tad thoughtfully, "that Major Peck might have known my own great, great, great grandfather, General Kosciuszko, or to give him his full name Tadeusz Andrizej Bonwentura Kosciuszko."

'Oh, Tad," Cynthia exclaimed, "that's where your name came from!"

"Yes," said Tad, "Tadeusz is too much for school teachers, so I have had to get along with Tad. And my middle initial is K. for you guess whom.

"By the way, sir," he continued, turning to the Deacon, "the General founded the Society of the Cincinnati of which you are a member. Actually, I suppose I am eligible for membership."

During this astounding revelation, the Deacon remained speechless from astonishment and chagrin. Now he recovered his composure and said heartily, "Of course, you are, and I shall be proud to be your sponsor. But how does all this come to be?"

"Naturally, it's a long story," said Tad. "You know about Kosciuszko coming to help in the Revolution. He was only 30 and after the war he returned to Poland and lived on the family estate. It was at that time that his daughter, only 17, married Comte Mietkiewicz, my ancestor. Then Poland, under the General's command as dictator, attempted to copy the American Revolution and win her freedom from Russia. She failed, and the General and the rest of the family fled Poland and came back here. Congress had granted him 500 acres in Ohio, and there they settled, but the General returned to Europe to work for Poland's freedom. My grandmother, tired of the rough frontier life, persuaded my grandfather to move to New England — and the family has been here almost half a century."

"I'd love to hear you speak Polish," broke in Cynthia.

"I can't speak a word of it," laughed Tad. "My grandfather insisted that as American citizens we speak the language of the country. He never lost his accent, but as he said he spoke 'polished' English."

Then turning to the Deacon, he smiled "Come out to the farm some day and I'll show you the Kosciuszko commission as general in the Continental Army."

A thought struck the Deacon.

"Have you a portrait of the General, Tad?" he inquired.

"Yes, sir, in full regimentals when he was dictator of Poland in 1794. When they escaped, they took it from the frame, rolled it, and brought it to the United States."

"We'll certainly be out soon," promised the Deacon and purposely he used the plural, and stretching out his hand "my apologies."

"Next time I'll bring you a hundred and twenty-eight cubic feet of four foot logs and you can do your own sawing," laughed Tad.

After Cynthia had seen him to the door, she returned to find her father seated at his desk, gazing thoughtfully at the portrait of Major Peck in its place of honor over the fireplace.

Cynthia sat down quietly, then said, "I like to hear Tad say Mietkiewicz."

Her father looked at her quizzically, then remarked, "Some people might think the name as good as Peck."

"I'm sure I shall prefer it," she murmured, and kissing her father lightly on the cheek, she ran out of the room.

The Deacon continued to look at the Major's portrait and as he did so it was metamorphosed into that of an imposing heroic figure in plumed helmet with a broad sash of vivid hues from shoulder to waist, the breast sparkling with jeweled decorations, and with a broad seriously handsome face in which he discerned the features of the young man who had just departed.